DOWN THE CLYDE

JACK HOUSE

DOWN
THE CLYDE

W. & R. CHAMBERS LTD.
EDINBURGH & LONDON

McCorquodale, Glasgow

CONTENTS SECTION ONE

CONTENTS SECTION TWO

INTRODUCTION

BEFORE YOU GO DOWN
THE CLYDE

IT always strikes me as odd that Prefaces and Introductions to books are the bits that are written last. That is the case here. But it does give an author the chance to sum up what he hopes he has done.

In " Down the Clyde " I have tried to provide a book which I don't think exists at present. There are guides to various parts of the Firth of Clyde. There are some excellent descriptive books about the Firth. In particular there is George Blake's " The Firth of Clyde," which, I should think, will remain the authoritative book on our estuary for many years to come. But it's not, of course, a guide to the Clyde in the customary sense.

I haven't attempted to compete with the experts or the literary lights, or even those industrious essayists who are ever on hand with a pretty piece on this most glorious part of Scotland. " Down the Clyde " is intended to be a practical guide to the whole area, from the Bridge Wharf, in the centre of Glasgow, to Campbeltown on the Highland side of the Firth and Ayr on the Lowland side.

While I have tried to pack as much information (geographical, historical and legendary!) as possible into this guide, the size of the book means that I have had to condense sometimes, and occasionally omit variations on a particular story. I often find the stories more interesting than the facts, but I think I've always made it clear which are which.

One word of warning. Things change on the Firth of Clyde. Steamers get old or too expensive, and have to go. The changing habits of holiday-makers sometimes mean changes in routes. Never accept anything I say as the last word. Check on sailings and trains and piers.

But, when I tell you about the Bocans and Bleaters in the Isle of Arran, or the ghost in Rothesay Castle, or the magic powers of Granny Kempock at Gourock, you can take it all as gospel!

JACK HOUSE.

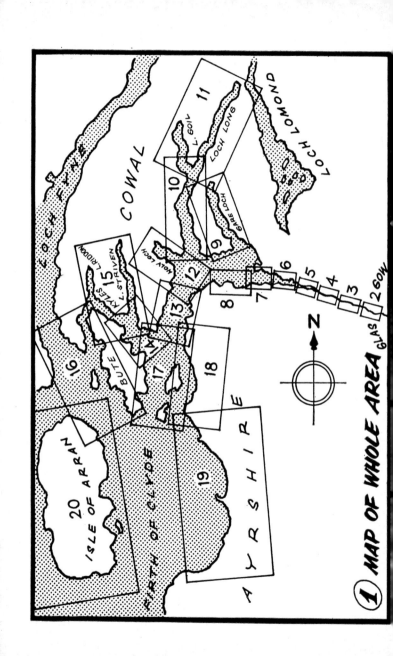

① MAP OF WHOLE AREA

MAP No. 1

THIS is a map of the whole area covered in this Guide Book. Each separate map which follows, from No. 2 to No. 20, is shown here in its relation to the entire *Firth of Clyde*. You can use each separate map in conjunction with this one to see just where you are on the Firth.

This map will also enable you to see the scale of the individual maps as opposed to the whole picture. We have patterned our maps not according to a set scale, but according to the amount of interest in each district. Thus you will see that each section of the River Clyde from the *Bridge Wharf in Glasgow* down to the Tail of the Bank gets as much space as the whole *Isle of Arran* or the *Gare Loch* or the *Ayrshire Coast*.

To use these maps properly, then, we'll imagine that you are sailing up *Loch Long* to *Arrochar* at its head. First you look at Map

No. 10 and then at this map, so that you see how the entrance to *Loch Long* fits into the whole scene. Then you go on to Map No. 11, having another look at this map to remind yourself of the geography.

This particular map may seem a little confusing to start with, but, after you've used it once or twice, you'll find it as clear as the sparkling water of the Clyde.

One feature we must specially point out. Each map shows the compass point to the North. So, to see exactly where you are, you should turn the page of the Guide Book to approximately North. This isn't difficult. If the sun is shining, and it's around the middle of the day, then the sun is about South. If the sun isn't shining, ask some bluff sea-dog aboard the steamer where the sun should be. These sailors have long memories, and he'll be able to tell you all right.

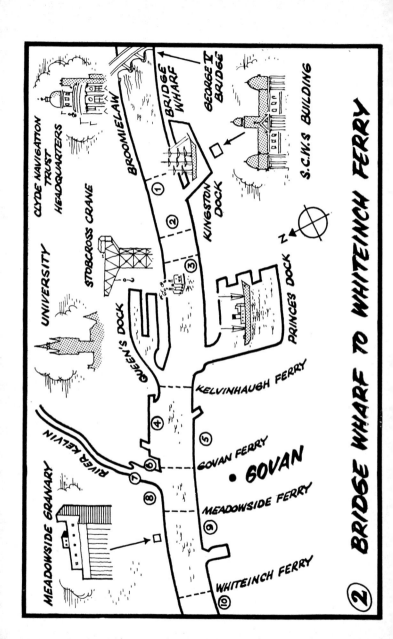

BRIDGE WHARF TO WHITEINCH FERRY

CLYDE NAVIGATION TRUST HEADQUARTERS

UNIVERSITY

STOBCROSS CRANE

BROOMIELAW

BRIDGE WHARF

GEORGE V BRIDGE

S.C.W.S BUILDING

KINGSTON DOCK

QUEEN'S DOCK

PRINCES DOCK

N

KELVINHAUGH FERRY

GOVAN FERRY

• GOVAN

MEADOWSIDE FERRY

WHITEINCH FERRY

RIVER KELVIN

MEADOWSIDE GRANARY

②

Every morning a steamer sails right down the river to the *Firth of Clyde*. We leave from Bridge Wharf, just by the George V Bridge (at the moment of writing, the newest bridge over the Clyde). Opposite is the famous Broomielaw, the first harbour of *Glasgow*. Behind the Broomielaw you see the dome of the Clyde Navigation Trust headquarters. The Clyde Trust controls the *Port of Glasgow*.

The steamers on the right are the Burns-Laird boats plying between *Glasgow* and *Ireland*. Right in front is the first of 11 ferries. This (1) is Clyde Street Ferry, and soon after we pass Kingston Dock, the first Glasgow wet dock, we come to (2) Finnieston Ferry. On the right is the Stobcross Crane, 175 tons, the biggest on the Clyde. Then (3) Stobcross Ferry.

On the right past Kelvinhaugh Ferry we see (4) Yorkhill Quay, where the Anchor Liners dock from *America* and *India*. The red building on the hill is the Royal Sick Children's Hospital.

And now we come to the start of the Clyde's great shipbuilding industry. More ships are built here than in any other one place in the world. On the left (5) is the shipyard of Harland & Wolff, Ltd.

Across the water, the River Kelvin flows into the Clyde and (6) at the confluence is Pointhouse Shipyard, belonging to A. & J. Inglis. Also on the Kelvin is (7) a graving dock and (8) D. & W. Henderson's ship repair yard.

Past Meadowside Ferry on the left (9) is the famous Fairfield Yard, and then (10) the Linthouse Yard belonging to Alex. Stephen & Sons, Ltd.

For fuller details, please turn to page 65

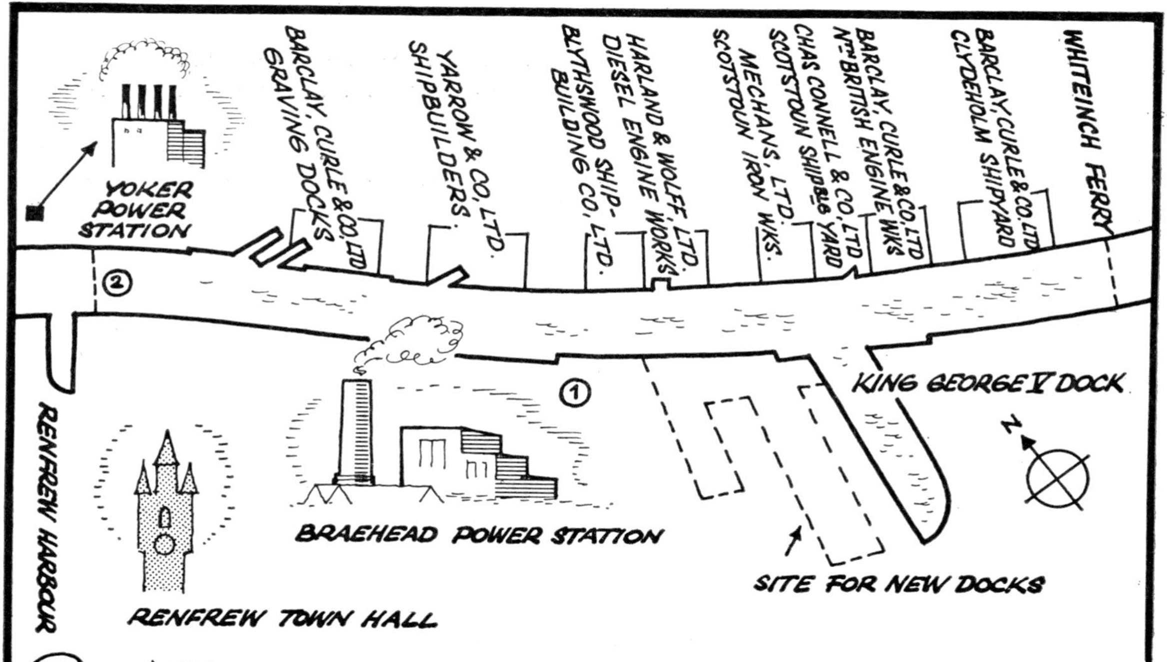

WHITEINCH FERRY TO YOKER FERRY

WHITEINCH FERRY

BARCLAY, CURLE & CO. LTD.
CLYDEHOLM SHIPYARD

BARCLAY, CURLE & CO. LTD.
Nth BRITISH ENGINE WKS.

CHAS CONNELL & CO. LTD.
SCOTSTOUN SHIPBLG. YARD

MECHANS, LTD.
SCOTSTOUN IRON WKS.

HARLAND & WOLFF, LTD.
DIESEL ENGINE WORKS

BLYTHSWOOD SHIP-
BUILDING CO., LTD.

YARROW & CO., LTD.
SHIPBUILDERS

BARCLAY, CURLE & CO. LTD.
GRAVING DOCKS

KING GEORGE II DOCK

SITE FOR NEW DOCKS

N

①

BRAEHEAD POWER STATION

RENFREW TOWN HALL

②

YOKER POWER STATION

RENFREW HARBOUR

③

MAP No. 3

Now here we are right in the heart of the Clyde shipbuilding industry and, to make things easier for you, we have given the names of the yards in full on the map. During World War II, the Clyde yards built or repaired at least 13 ships a day for five years. They still build the biggest and best ships in the world here.

Most of the shipbuilding yards are on the right. On the left you see the King George V Dock, opened in 1931. The waste ground alongside is destined to be turned into new docks, and then comes (1) one of the few shipbuilding firms on the south side of the river at this point—Blythswood Shipbuilding Co., Ltd. The main yard is just opposite, on the other side of the river.

The chimney of Braehead Power Station on the left is said to have the broadest diameter of any chimney in Europe. It has special lighting to warn off aircraft taking off or landing at *Renfrew Airport* (which serves the *City of Glasgow*), just on the other side of the Power Station.

There are some small shipbuilding firms around *Renfrew Harbour*, which is just past Renfrew (or Yoker) Ferry (2). Both these names are used for this ferry, but you will realise that *Yoker* is on the North and *Renfrew* is on the South.

We are now sailing out of *Glasgow*. The right bank is still *Glasgow* until the steamer passes Yoker Power Station. The left bank ceased to be Glasgow as we approached Braehead Power Station. At this point the city boundary is the middle of the River Clyde.

For fuller details, please turn to page 70

ROTHESAY DOCK TO ERSKINE FERRY

(4)

Labels within the illustration:
- N (compass)
- ROTHESAY DOCK
- RIVER CART
- SINGER'S CLOCK
- SINGER
- JOHN BROWN & Co. LTD CLYDEBANK SHIPYARD
- ST PATRICK
- FORTH AND CLYDE CANAL
- OLD KILPATRICK
- OIL WHARVES
- NEWSHOT ISLE
- PARK QUAY
- ERSKINE FERRY
- THE QUEEN ELIZABETH

MAP No. 4

Get your camera ready, for we are now approaching John Brown's shipyard, from which the two biggest ships in the world were launched—the "Queen Mary" and the "Queen Elizabeth". The river here is so narrow that it would not be possible to launch ships of such a size if it were not for the River Cart, which flows into the Clyde just opposite John Brown's.

When an 80,000-ton ship is launched, she follows the dotted line on the map right up the Cart, and is then pulled back into the Clyde by tugs.

There is a thriving shipbuilding yard up the River Cart at *Paisley*, which is more renowned, perhaps, for being the world centre for thread-making.

The town behind John Brown's is *Clyde-bank*, the most severely blitzed place in Scotland during World War II. Look for Singer's clock. It is the world's largest clock-face, almost 30 feet in diameter.

Past Newshot Isle the wrecks you see on the shore to the left are, like the boat-houses at Park Quay, relics of a World War II scrap depot.

Erskine Ferry is the last of the 11 ferries of the River Clyde. It connects *Dunbarton-shire* on the right with *Renfrewshire* on the left.

The high ground in the background on the right is part of the *Kilpatrick Hills*, and the houses there are the first of the village of *Old Kilpatrick*. According to Scottish legend, St. Patrick, the patron Saint of Ireland was born here. The Irish disagree, but you can see St. Patrick's Well in the village.

For fuller details, please turn to page 72

(5) OLD KILPATRICK TO DUMBUCK

OLD KILPATRICK
FORTH & CLYDE CANAL
ST. PATRICK'S STONE
BOWLING HARBOUR
HENRY BELL MONUMENT
DUMBUCK
ERSKINE HOUSE
HENRY BELL MONUMENT
LONG DYKE
N

You have just seen the benign St. Patrick. Now look upon his sworn enemy, the De'il himsel'! Auld Nick was the reason that St. Patrick left Scotland for Ireland. The story is that, when the De'il saw the holy man escaping from the Clyde, he tore a great rock from the top of Dumbuck Hill and threw it at St. Patrick. It missed the saint and fell in the river, and you see it there in front of you, with a warning light on the top of it, plainly marked "St. Patrick's Stone."

On the left stands Erskine House, once a ducal residence, but now the Princess Louise Scottish Hospital for Limbless Sailors and Soldiers.

On the right, *Bowling Harbour* is the entrance to the *Forth and Clyde Canal*, which runs 35 miles across Scotland to the Firth of Forth. *Bowling* is the meeting-place of four forms of transport, for side by side are the river, the railway, the canal and the road.

Henry Bell's monument stands in the grounds of Dunglass Castle, once the seat of the Colquhouns of Luss. Henry Bell sailed his steamer, the "Comet," on the Clyde in August, 1812, and so is credited with having introduced steam navigation to Europe.

If, as the steamer sails on, you look back across the country to the South, you'll see a twin of the Henry Bell monument on that side.

Past *Dunglass* on the left you will see the remains of the Long Dyke, an invention of John Golborne of Chester, the engineer who first deepened the Clyde and made it possible for ships to sail right up to Glasgow. The Long Dyke runs down to opposite Dumbarton Rock.

For fuller details, please turn to page 74

HIRAM WALKER & SONS (SCOTLAND) LTD DISTILLERY

DUMBARTON ROCK

DUMBARTON PARK

LONG DYKE

LANGBANK

FINLAYSTON HOUSE

KEIL SCHOOL

FINLAYSTON POINT

☐ FINLAYSTON POINT

N

⑥ DUMBARTON ROCK TO FINLAYSTON POINT

MAP No. 6

On our right is *Dumbarton Rock*, and the building you can see at the foot of it is Dumbarton Castle. The Rock is 260 feet high and a mile in circumference. It has been a coign of vantage to the Caledonians, the Romans, the Knights of the Round Table, Mary Queen of Scots, and her adversaries. (The story of Dumbarton Rock is told on page 77).

The river which joins the *Clyde* here is the *Leven*, flowing from Loch Lomond. On its banks is one of the most famous Clyde ship-building firms, Denny's. If you are sailing on the "Queen Mary II," you'll be interested to know she was built at Denny's.

The town behind the rock is *Dumbarton*, and the big group of red buildings is the second largest Scotch whisky distillery in the world, Hiram Walker's. If the visibility is good, you will see *Ben Lomond* just behind *Dumbarton*.

The steamer is now sailing out of the *River Clyde* and into the *Firth*, and keeps to the Southern, or left shore. On the right, just past the trees of Dumbarton Park, and sur-rounded by new council houses, is Keil School, a public school for Highland boys and boys especially interested in agriculture.

On the left you see Finlayston House up on the hill. The Earl of Glencairn, who lived here in the 16th century, was the first Scottish noble to become a Protestant, and John Knox preached in that house.

You'll see trains on each side of the river. Those on the North are running to *Helens-burgh* and the *Highlands*. On the South they are going to the main ports for seeing the *Firth of Clyde*.

For further details please turn to page 77.

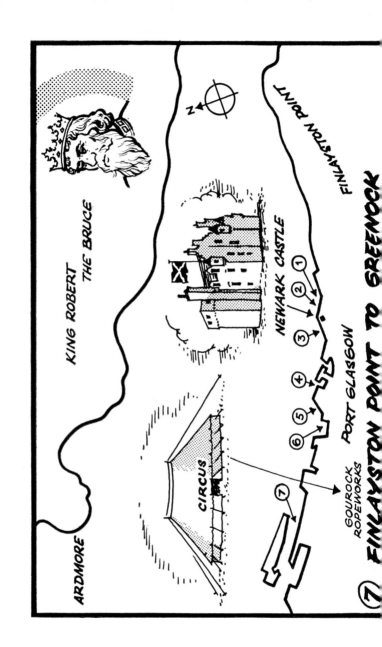

KING ROBERT THE BRUCE

ARDMORE

CIRCUS

NEWARK CASTLE

PORT GLASGOW

GOUROCK ROPEWORKS

FINLAYSTON POINT

N

① ② ③ ④ ⑤ ⑥ ⑦

⑦ FINLAYSTON POINT TO GREENOCK

On the right and to the West the houses you see are those of the village of *Cardross*. Between *Dumbarton* and *Cardross* stood the castle where Robert the Bruce died in 1329. By defeating Edward II's much bigger army at Bannockburn in 1314, Bruce set the seal on the independence of Scotland.

The King finished his life here and often sailed across these waters, for he had ships specially built for him at *Dumbarton*.

The steamer keeps to the left and you'll see the wooden stumps which show the outlines of the timber ponds going back to the days when *Port Glasgow* did a big timber trade with America.

Port Glasgow is an important shipbuilding centre. You'll see (1) the shipbreaking yard of Smith and Houston; (2) Lamont's shipyard; Newark Castle, an old stronghold of the Maxwell family now open to the public;

(3) Ferguson Brothers' shipyard; (4) Lithgow's East Yard; (5) William Hamilton's shipyard; and (6) Lithgow's Kingston Yard.

The big red building behind the Port Glasgow waterfront is the Gourock Ropeworks, a firm which has supplied ropes to the whole world. Besides making the ropes for the "Queen Mary" and the "Queen Elizabeth," they have made several Big Tops for Bertram Mills' Circus.

Port Glasgow was originally built as the harbour of *Glasgow* by the city merchants in 1668. When the river was deepened up to *Glasgow*, the town lost its place as a harbour and turned to shipbuilding.

Port Glasgow merges into *Greenock* and (7) we sail past the entrance to the Great Harbour of Greenock.

For fuller details, please turn to page 79

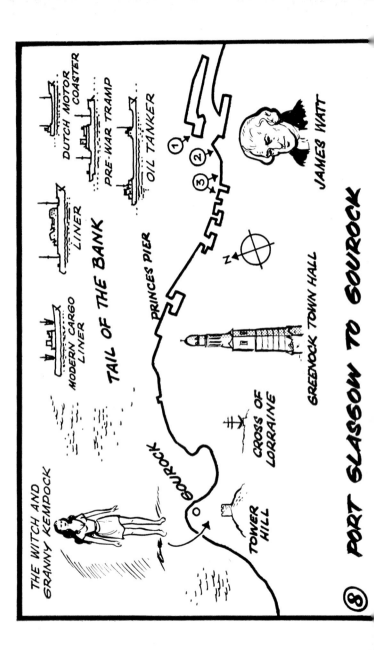

THE WITCH AND GRANNY KEMPOCK

DUTCH MOTOR COASTER

PRE-WAR TRAMP

OIL TANKER

LINER

MODERN CARGO LINER

TAIL OF THE BANK

PRINCES PIER

JAMES WATT

GREENOCK TOWN HALL

CROSS OF LORRAINE

TOWER HILL

GOUROCK

⑧ PORT GLASGOW TO GOUROCK

MAP No. 8

We sail past the *Great Harbour of Greenock* and see (1) the Garvel Shipyard of George Brown & Co. (no relation to John Brown of Clydebank); and then (2) the Greenock Dockyard Co., and (3) Scott's shipbuilding yard, belonging to the oldest firm of shipbuilders in the world. The first Scotts launched fishing boats in 1771, and the firm is still a family concern.

Now we are approaching the Tail of the Bank, the end of the sandbank which runs down the Clyde from *Dumbarton* to *Greenock*. This is a world-famous anchorage, and it was particularly important during World War II. To help you to recognise vessels which may be at anchor at the Tail of the Bank, we show you a number of typical outlines of ships seen in the Firth.

Rising out of the middle of *Greenock* you see the Italianate tower of Greenock Town Hall. Greenock is the birthplace of the great inventor, James Watt, and also, of the notorious pirate, Captain Kidd.

The houses run straight on from *Greenock* to the holiday resort of *Gourock*, one of the important cruising steamer ports of the Clyde. The steamer crosses Cardwell Bay and you'll see the Cross of Lorraine on the hill between *Greenock and Gourock*. This is a World War II memorial to the Free French Naval Forces. On the hill behind *Gourock* is an old watch-tower.

The pier is built at Kempock Point, and in *Gourock* you will see "Granny Kempock," a stone which had magic powers for sailors. A teen-age girl was burned at the stake as a witch in 1662 when she confessed that the witches planned to throw "Granny Kempock" into the Clyde.

For fuller details, please turn to page 85

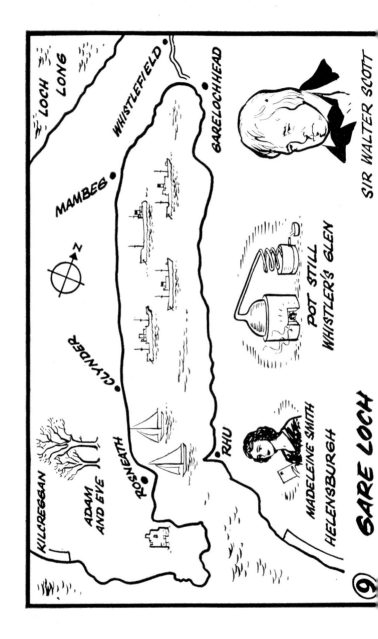

LOCH LONG

WHISTLEFIELD

GARELOCHHEAD

MAMBEG

SIR WALTER SCOTT

N

CLYNDER

POT STILL
WHISTLER'S GLEN

KILCREGGAN

ROSNEATH

RHU

ADAM AND EVE

MADELEINE SMITH
HELENSBURGH

⑨ GARE LOCH

If you have been following these maps consecutively, note the change of direction in this one. North has been pointing to the top of the page. Now it points to the right. Up till now points of interest have been described from right to left on the map. There are occasional cruises up the *Gare Loch*, but most people travel round the loch by road, so our description takes the same route—from *Helensburgh* up to *Garelochhead*, then down the other side to *Rosneath* and *Kilcreggan.*

Helensburgh has a pier at *Craigendoran,* which serves most of the Clyde. The town (a holiday resort) was named after his wife by Sir James Colquhoun of Luss. Here were born Henry Bell, who started steam navigation in Europe, Jack Buchanan, the musical comedy star; and J. L. Baird, the pioneer of television.

One of the most famous murder cases has a connection with Rhu, because Madeleine Smith had a holiday house there.

Sir Walter Scott used this countryside as part of the background for his "Heart of Midlothian." Near Rhu is the Whistler's Glen, famous for secret whisky stills. King George IV tasted whisky from an illicit pot still operating here.

Rhu is famous for yachting, but past it you see the "mothballed" Navy and an enormous shipbreaking yard. Up from *Garelochhead, Whistlefield* has a startling view, looking down the *Gare Loch* and across at *Loch Long* and *Loch Goil.*

Small villages down the other side of the *Gare Loch* lead to *Rosneath,* where there are two ancient trees known as "Adam and Eve."

For fuller details, please turn to pages 92, 84

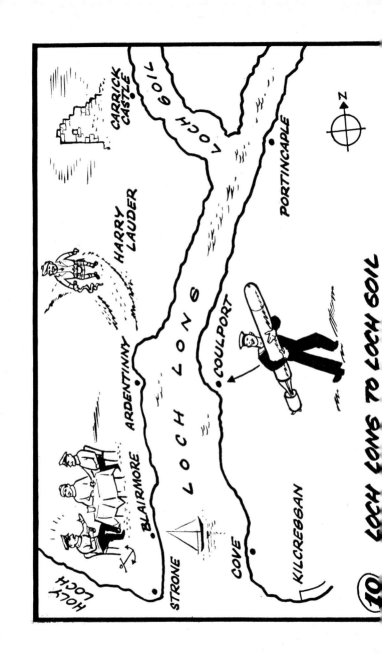

10 LOCH LONG TO LOCH GOIL

MAP No. 10

Once again, note that in this map North is to the right. Since you are sailing up *Loch Long*, places and points of interest are described from left to right.

Loch Long and *Loch Goil* are the fiords of the Firth of Clyde, and the entrance to the 20 miles from the Firth to *Arrochar* are guarded by the twin villages of *Kilcreggan* and *Cove* on the East and *Strone* on the West.

The small yachts sail out from Blairmore because one of the sailing schools run by the National Council for Physical Recreation is based there.

On the right there is a strange 'H'-shaped erection near *Coulport*. *Loch Long* is much used by the Admiralty, and that is an Admiralty ballistic testing station.

The next place past *Blairmore* on the left is *Ardentinny*, made famous by Harry Lauder's song—"Ower the hill tae Ardentinny, just tae see ma bonnie Jeannie." Behind *Ardentinny* is *Glen Finart*, and the road that Harry Lauder said he took, runs up over the hill and down to *Loch Eck*, on the other side of the mountain.

The Paisley poet, Tannahill, wrote the first song about Jeannie and Ardentinny, and the white building near the shore is the inn where he met her.

State forests cover the hillside to the left, and the buildings past *Ardentinny* belong to the Forestry Commission. At Bird Point we come to the entrance to *Loch Goil* and sail up past Carrick Castle, considered impregnable until the men of Athole besieged and burned it in 1685.

For fuller details, please turn to page 100

c

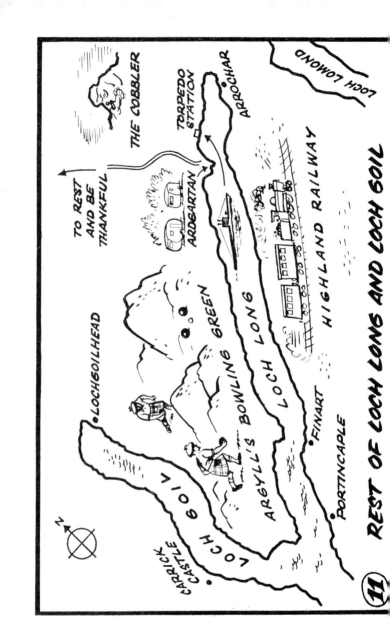

REST OF LOCH LONG AND LOCH GOIL

MAP No. 11

Loch Goil is **not** the Loch Goil of Thomas Campbell's famous poem, "Lord Ullin's Daughter." (It's in the Isle of Mull). We sail up to the village of *Lochgoilhead*. The mountainside behind *Lochgoilhead* is a Glasgow public park! It is the 15,000-acre Ardgoil Park, given to the city by the late Lord Rowallan in 1906.

We sail back down *Loch Goil* and into *Loch Long* again, and by mountains which are known as Argyll's Bowling Green. On the right is the oil port of *Finnart*, where ocean-going oil tankers can unload their cargo. Above the road you may see a train climbing up the track of the West Highland Railway.

On the left there is an occasional house, where 200 houses once stood. The houses were emptied and destroyed at the time of the Highland Clearances.

The caravans and tents you see on the left mark *Ardgartan*, the first camping site to be developed in Britain.

The rafts in the loch belong to the torpedo testing station, and red flags show that Admiralty tests are being carried out. You see the station itself just past *Ardgartan* on the left.

The steamer comes into Arrochar Pier. *Arrochar* is a holiday resort, and a road leads over to *Tarbet* on the shore of *Loch Lomond*, only a little over a mile away.

Another road leads round the top of *Loch Long* and over the *Rest and be Thankful* to *Loch Fyne*, with a connection also to Dunoon by *Loch Eck*. From here you'll see the famous *Cobbler*, the 2,891-foot mountain which is famous among climbers.

For fuller details, please turn to page 102

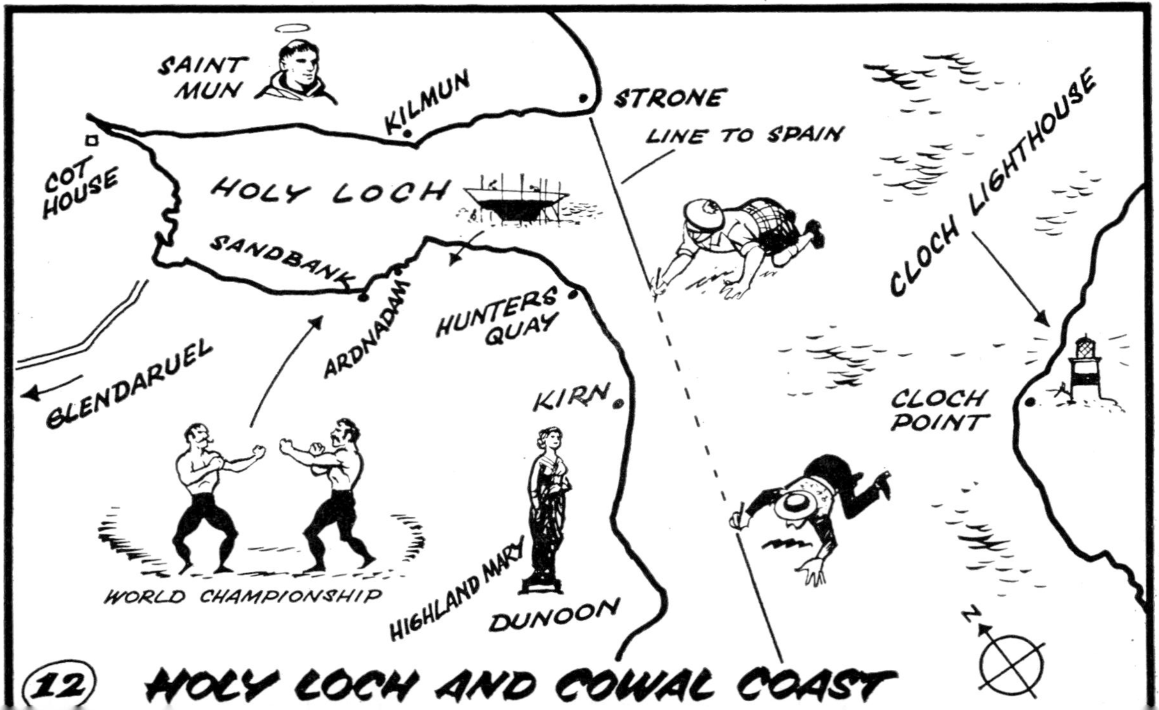

(12) HOLY LOCH AND COWAL COAST

SAINT MUN

COT HOUSE

KILMUN

HOLY LOCH

SANDBANK

STRONE

LINE TO SPAIN

GLENDARUEL

ARDNADAM

HUNTERS QUAY

KIRN

WORLD CHAMPIONSHIP

HIGHLAND MARY

DUNOON

CLOCH LIGHTHOUSE

CLOCH POINT

N

MAP No. 12

You may be sailing across the Firth of Clyde from *Gourock* (just North of the Cloch Lighthouse), or you may be going round the Cowal Coast by road. Either way, you start reading this map from *Strone* at the top and follow the coastline.

They say that, if you draw a line from Strone Point in a South-South-Westerly direction, it won't touch land until it arrives at Spain.

The Holy Loch is said to take its name from St. Mun, who settled at Kilmun. The mausoleum in the Kilmun kirkyard is where the Dukes of Argyll are buried.

The Cot House Inn is at the top of the loch, where the *River Echaig* flows from *Loch Eck*. The main road continues by the coast, but there is a road to the West, leading to *Glendaruel*.

Sandbank on the coast road is famous for yacht-building, and the ill-starred "Sceptre," beaten by the "Columbia" in the America's Cup races, was built there. Behind the coast villages is the Cowal Golf Course, where the bare-knuckle championship of Britain was fought in the middle of last century.

Hunter's Quay is the headquarters of the Royal Clyde Yacht Club. *Kirn* is a holiday resort, and now part of the *Burgh of Dunoon*— one of the biggest holiday places on the Firth of Clyde.

Behind Dunoon Pier to the left you will see the statue of Highland Mary, looking across to *Ayrshire*. She was beloved by Robert Burns, but died young. She was born at Auchamore, just behind Dunoon.

For fuller details, please turn to page 107

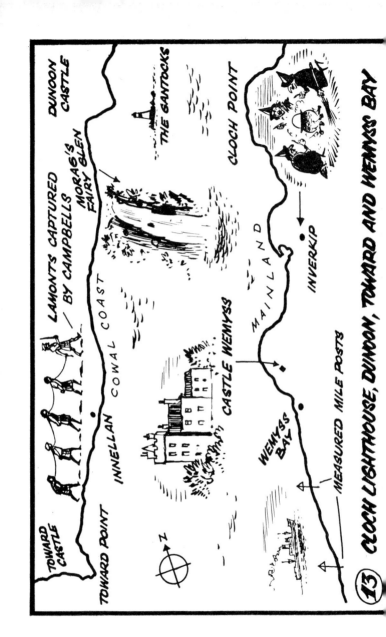

CLOCH LIGHTHOUSE, DUNOON, TOWARD AND WEMYSS' BAY

13

MAP No. 13

This map should be read from right to left along the *Cowal Coast* at the top, and from left to right along the mainland at the foot. This corresponds with most steamer sailing routes.

Just behind the statue of Highland Mary at *Dunoon* is the site of Dunoon Castle. Don't mistake Dunoon Town Council Chambers for the Castle. It was built in 1822 by Lord Provost Ewing of Glasgow as a seaside house.

Watch out for a long white house on the shore. It once belonged to Sir Harry Lauder. You will see the Bathing Lido near it. Behind the Lido is Morag's Fairy Glen, a beauty spot with a popular ballad attached to it. *Innellan* is a holiday resort, and the place where a blind minister wrote the famous hymn, "O, love that will not let me go."

A lighthouse at *Toward Point* marks where the steamer turns into *Rothesay Bay*. Behind it are the ruins of Toward Castle, once the seat of the Lamonts. In 1646 the Campbells who held Dunoon Castle, got possession of Toward Castle by a trick, and took the Lamonts to Dunoon, where they were murdered.

Across from *Toward Point* is *Wemyss Bay*, the main port for *Rothesay*. Just South of *Wemyss Bay* is the *Measured Mile* where new ships are tested for speed. Just north is Castle Wemyss which belonged to the late Lord Inverclyde.

The village between *Wemyss Bay* and the *Cloch Lighthouse* is *Inverkip*, where the last witches in the West of Scotland were burned in 1662.

For fuller details, please turn to pages 111, 90

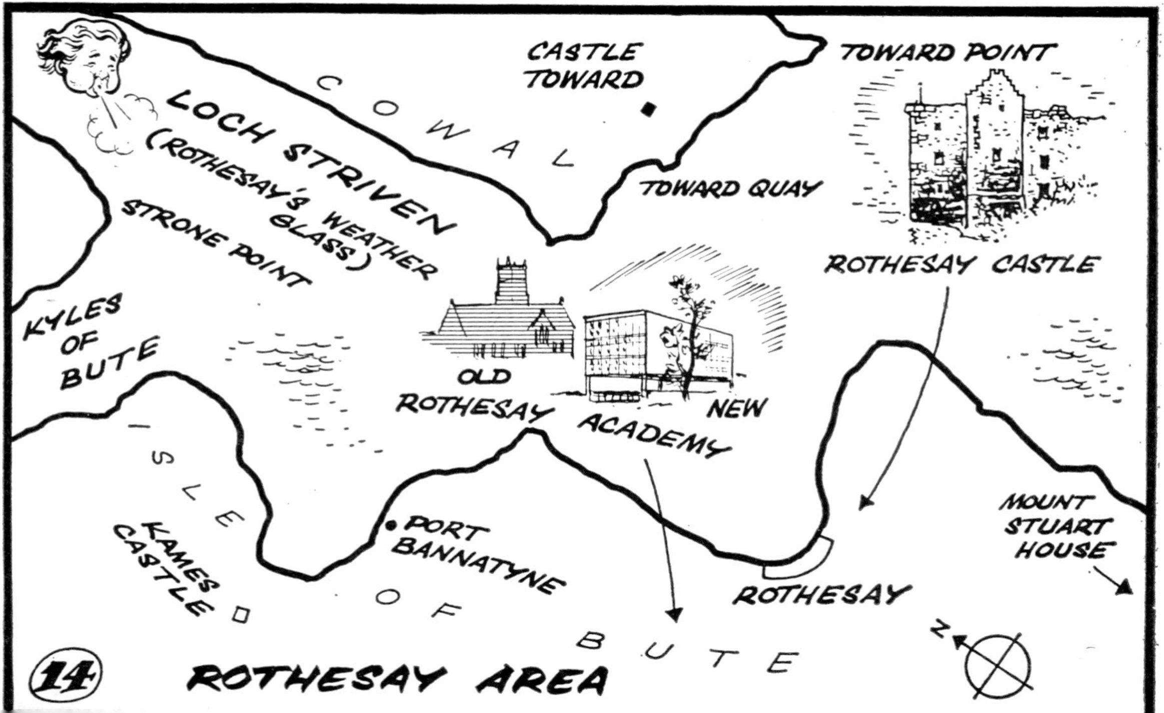

ROTHESAY AREA

TOWARD POINT

ROTHESAY CASTLE

MOUNT STUART HOUSE →

ROTHESAY

TOWARD QUAY

CASTLE TOWARD

C O W A L

LOCH STRIVEN
(ROTHESAY'S WEATHER GLASS)

STRONE POINT

NEW ACADEMY

OLD ROTHESAY ACADEMY

PORT BANNATYNE

I S L E   O F   B U T E

KYLES OF BUTE

KAMES CASTLE

N

14

The steamer sails into sweet *Rothesay Bay* by *Toward Point* and across to the *Madeira of Scotland, Rothesay*. Up to the hill to the West of the town is the new Rothesay Academy, replacing the Victorian one which was set on fire by three pupils a few years ago!

Just behind Rothesay pier and its line of hotels is Rothesay Castle, said to have been founded by the Viking, Magnus Barefoot, in the 11th century. The Castle is now a ruin, but it was in it that Robert II of Scotland made his son Duke of Rothesay. That is one of the titles of the Prince of Wales to-day.

The promenade to the East goes to Mount Stuart House, home of the Marquis of Bute, who owns the Isle of Bute.

To the West, *Rothesay* links up with *Port Bannatyne*, round *Ardbeg Point*. In the summer the South Georgian whalers lie up in Kames Bay here. Inland is the 14th century Kames Castle and behind it Wester Kames, a peel tower said to be the oldest inhabited house in Scotland.

Across on the *Cowal Coast*, just past *Toward Point*, you will see Castle Toward (not to be confused with the ruins of Toward Castle, seen in Map No. 13). This mansion was built by Lord Provost Kirkman Finlay of Glasgow, and is now used by Glasgow Corporation as a holiday school for Glasgow children.

When you are sailing through the *Kyles of Bute*, the steamer's route takes you between *Kames Bay and Loch Striven*. This lonely loch is called "Rothesay's Weather Glass" because, whatever the weather is like in *Loch Striven*, it will be the same 15 minutes later in *Rothesay*.

For fuller details, please turn to page 128

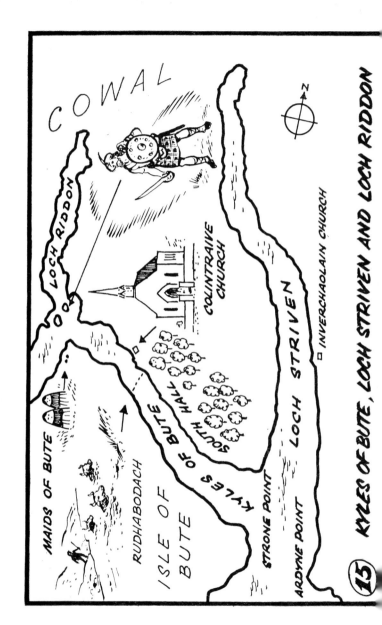

15 KYLES OF BUTE, LOCH STRIVEN AND LOCH RIDDON

MAP No. 15

Note the change in the North point, as compared with Map No. 14 if you are travelling by steamer. *Loch Striven* runs North, but the steamer turns West and then South round the dog-leg of the *Kyles of Bute.*

Loch Striven is used by the Admiralty as a submarine testing site. Only occasional cruises take you up the loch.

The steamers enter the *Kyles (meaning "Narrows") of Bute* between the *Isle of Bute* on the left and the *Cowal Coast* on the right.

The first large house on the right is South Hall, and the woods round it were planted to represent the formations of the British and French armies at the Battle of Waterloo. Most of the trees were destroyed by Norwegian Commandos training here.

As we near the village of *Colintraive* we see the little kirk. Ask any of the sailors on the steamer what's unusual about it.

Colintraive means "the swimming narrows" and where you see the ferry crossing at Rhudabodach, is the place where the Highlanders swam their cattle to and from Bute.

As the steamer turns by *Loch Riddon*, watch out for a small island with a single tree growing on it, off the Cowal shore. It is *Eilean Dheirg* ("Red Island"), and it was fortified by the earl of Argyll in 1685, when he was fighting against King James II. Three Government frigates attacked and took the island, and Argyll had to flee.

When the steamer turns South, look to the left at the *Isle of Bute* for the *Maids of Bute,* two boulders on the hillside painted to resemble two old ladies in Welsh dress.

For fuller details, please turn to page 137

16 ARDLAMONT, WEST SIDE OF BUTE TO GARROCH HEAD

MAP No. 16

The customary *Kyles of Bute* cruise ends at *Tighnabruaich* (Gaelic for "the house on the brae"—an inn which stood on the hillside above the pier). Time allowed on shore, then the steamer sails back to *Glasgow*.

When the cruise continues, we have the *Ardlamont peninsula* on the right and the *Isle of Bute* on the left. The grounds of Ardlamont House stretch towards the point, but the House itself is seen from the Loch Fyne side. In these grounds occurred the famous "Ardlamont Mystery," when A. J. Monson was charged with murdering his pupil in 1893. The charge was found "Not Proven," a verdict peculiar to Scotland.

When we reach *Ettrick Bay* we have travelled 15 miles round the Northern half of the *Isle of Bute*, but the distance from *Ettrick Bay* to *Rothesay* is only three miles.

Inchmarnock is the "calf" of Bute, and is also known as the Drunkard's Isle because the people of Bute marooned their alcoholics there in days gone by.

There are excellent bathing beaches on this side of *Bute*. Between one of them, *Scalpsie Bay*, and *Garroch Head* some distance inland is St. Blane's Chapel, where there are two cemeteries. St. Blane ordered that men only should be buried in the higher one and women in the lower one. This was because, when he was transporting holy earth to his chapel, the back-band on one of his horses broke. He asked a fisherwoman for her belt, but she would not give it so the saint took his revenge by banning women from the high cemetery. St Blane made this order in the 11th century and it was not disobeyed until the 17th century.

For fuller details, please turn to page 133

17 TOWARD PT. TO GARROCH HEAD WITH THE CUMBRAES

MAP No. 17

This map has a dual purpose—to show, after Maps 14, 15 and 16, the rest of the cruise round the *Isle of Bute*; and the *Great and Little Cumbrae Islands*, which are usually reached from *Largs* on the mainland.

Rounding *Garroch Head* the steamer sails past *Kilchattan Bay*, a small holiday resort where the pier is to be rebuilt by the Admiralty. The grounds of Mount Stuart, the home of the Marquis of Bute, cover much of this part of Bute. Soon we are again in *Rothesay Bay*.

In 1263 the *Firth of Clyde* from *Bute* across to the mainland was swarming with the warships of King Haakon of Norway. The Vikings were defeated at the Battle of Largs, and many of their dead were buried on the *Cumbrae Islands*.

The *Great Cumbrae* is 3½ miles long and 11 miles round. Approaching it from *Largs* (just below the lion's head) you see the Lion Rock, on the shore and then Keppel Pier with the Scottish Marine Biological Station behind it. In the attached museum you will see live examples of every kind of marine creature in the *Firth of Clyde*, including an octopus.

Millport is a very popular holiday resort and has three fine bathing beaches. On one of them is the Crocodile Rock painted to resemble the crocodile in "Peter Pan." Behind Millport promenade is the Cathedral of Argyll and the Isles, consecrated in 1879 (Episcopal Church).

The *Little Cumbrae* is visited by boat from *Millport*. There is only a farm on it and beside the farm are the remains of a castle destroyed by Cromwell. The tower on the top was once the first lighthouse in the Firth. Built in 1775, it was really a coal fire in a huge grate.

For fuller details, please turn to page 122

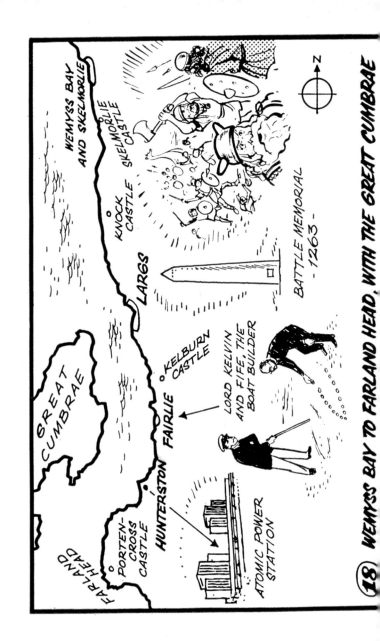

(18) WEMYSS BAY TO FARLAND HEAD, WITH THE GREAT CUMBRAE

In this map, once again, read from right to left.

Wemyss Bay is the main port for *Rothesay* and is a twin village to *Skelmorlie*, opposite which ships run their trials on the Measured Mile. From *Wemyss Bay* steamers also sail to *Largs* and *Millport* on the *Great Cumbrae*. From the deck you will see Skelmorlie Castle and later Knock Castle. From *Skelmorlie* on the mainland is *Ayrshire.*

Largs is a noted holiday resort, and the home of the Royal Largs Yacht Club. The new sport here is sailing catamarans.

At *Largs* in 1263 the Scots defeated the Vikings and ended their rule in the Islands and the West of Scotland. A monument shows where the Vikings were finally defeated. Owing to its shape it is known locally as "The Pencil."

We pass Kelburn Castle, the home of the Earl of Glasgow, and reach *Fairlie*, another Clyde port and famous for yachts and yacht-building. Fife of Fairlie and Lord Kelvin designed yachts on the shore. These yachts were built, and the boat-builder's always beat the scientist's. *Fairlie* is to be the site of a N.A.T.O. defence boom.

The ultra-modern buildings of Hunterston Nuclear Power Station are on Hunterston Estate, just past Fairlie. The nuclear power to be made here is to be for peaceful purposes.

At *Farland Head* the ruined building is Portencross Castle, with the clachan of Portencross behind it. The castle was built in the 12th century and is supposed to be the twin of the one across the water on the *Little Cumbrae.* (See Map No. 17).

For fuller details, please turn to page 117

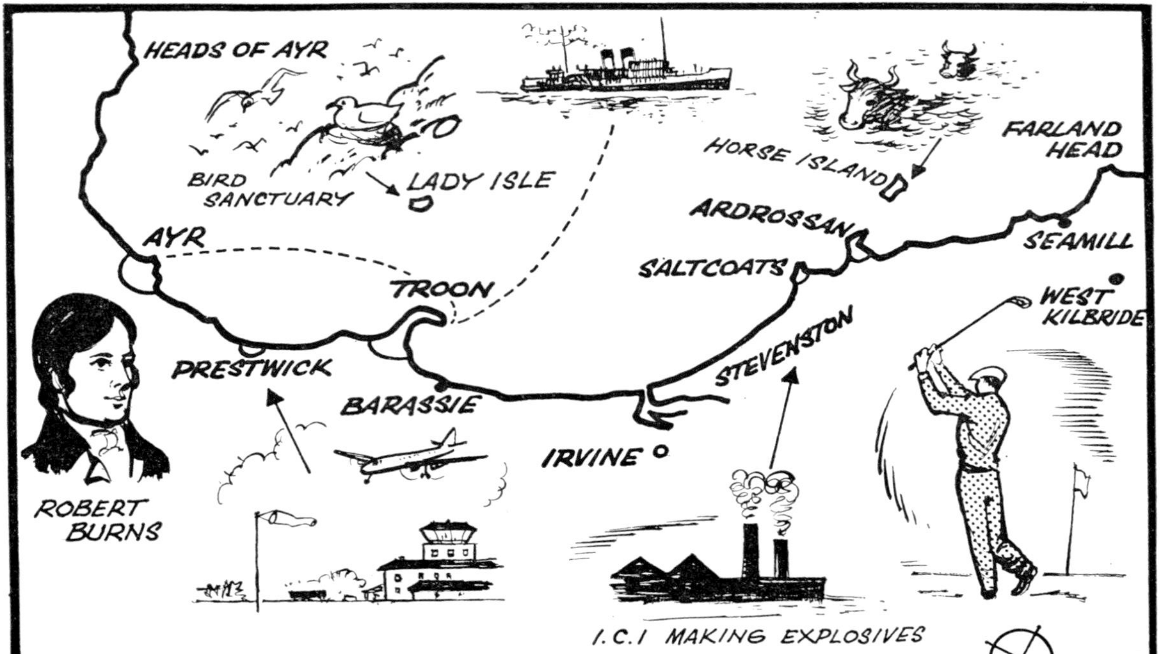

FARLAND HEAD

SEAMILL

WEST KILBRIDE

HORSE ISLAND

ARDROSSAN

SALTCOATS

STEVENSTON

IRVINE °

I.C.I MAKING EXPLOSIVES

HEADS OF AYR

LADY ISLE

BIRD SANCTUARY

TROON

BARASSIE

PRESTWICK

AYR

ROBERT BURNS

(18) *FARLAND HEAD TO AYR*

MAP No. 19

From *Farland Head* to *Ayr* there are 20 golf courses, an average of one per mile The first is the *West Kilbride* course on the shore between *Portencross* and *Seamill*, a popular place for football teams in training.

Ardrossan is one of the chief ports of the *Firth of Clyde* and serves *Arran, Ireland* and the *Isle of Man.* Off the shore is *Horse Island,* to which Ardrossan "cowboys" take cattle for the summer. The cattle swim ashore from boats.

Saltcoats is a popular holiday town, especially for day trippers from Glasgow. At *Stevenston* nearly four miles of the coastline and a large hinterland are occupied by the Ardeer Works of Imperial Chemical Industries and high explosives and many other things are made here.

Irvine is one of the oldest ports of the Clyde and is now a go-ahead industrial town. The oldest horse-race in the world is run here in August.

Troon is a holiday resort, shipbuilding centre and port. Off Troon is *Lady Isle*, a bird sanctuary leased at a rent of half-a-crown per year.

Prestwick is another holiday resort, but is also an international airport. It is the only fog-free airport in the British Isles, and has services to all parts of the world.

Ayr is a fine county town with a population of 50,000. It is the centre of the *Burns Country.* Over 100,000 people visit Burn's Cottage near *Ayr* every year. It has been visited by the Queen, Malenkov, Clark Gable, Irving Berlin and the Duke of Windsor.

For fuller details, please turn to page 143

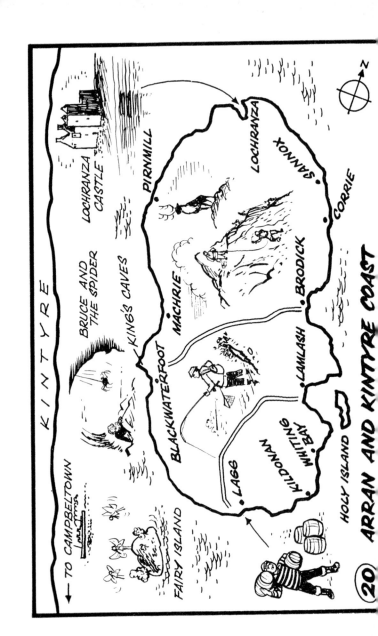

ARRAN AND KINTYRE COAST

20

Arran is the largest island in the *Firth of Clyde*. *Brodick* is the principal pier, but you can also land at *Lochranza* and *Whiting Bay*.

We follow the customary "Round the Island" Tour (60 miles) from *Brodick* North. Behind *Brodick* is the String Road, so-called because sailors liken it to a piece of string laid up the hillside.

Behind Brodick Castle (open to the public) is *Goatfell* and a stretch of wild mountains, giving some fine climbing. The road leads along the shore to *Corrie* (famous for artists) and over the hill to *Lochranza*. Watch out for deer—there are over 5,000 on the island.

Lochranza Castle was a hunting seat of the Scottish Kings. Near-by was the cottage owned by the grandparents of Prime Minister Macmillan.

From *Lochranza* it's a shore road again by *Pirnmill* and *Machrie* to *Blackwaterfoot*.

Here are the King's Caves. The King is Robert the Bruce and he is supposed to have seen the spider here.

If you are sailing round the South and see an island not marked on the map, don't land on it. It's a Fairy Island and you'll never get off again !

Lagg at the extreme South has palm trees growing in the open, and was once a smuggling centre for contraband between Scotland and Ireland. There is good fishing between *Lagg* and *Machrie*. The only other road across the island runs from *Lagg* to *Lamlash*.

By the shore there are holiday places at *Kildonan* and *Whiting Bay*. *Lamlash Bay* was where the Viking fleet gathered after the Battle of Largs in 1263. Off *Lamlash* is *Holy Isle*, once the residence of St. Molios and now owned by an American millionaire.

For fuller details, please turn to page 160

HIGH ROAD . . .

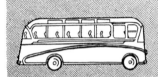

OR LOW ROAD . . .

It's all the more enjoyable travelling in a DODDS SUPER COACH. Being the largest Private Coach Operators in the West of Scotland, we offer a superlative service to

CLUBS—GUILDS and all PRIVATE PARTIES

who wish to make the most of their outings.

Whatever the number — the distance — we will be pleased to quote.

TOURS throughout the season to the Historic and Beauty Spots in Scotland.

See Local Press for details.

Next Time — Travel in Style —

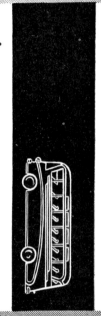

GO DODDS COACHES

72 Portland St., TROON
Telephone: 97 (3 lines)

CHAPTER ONE

WELCOME TO THE CLYDE

THE River Clyde is one of the best known and most remarkable waterways in the world. From its source in the lonely Lowther Hills to the teeming harbour of Glasgow is not much more than a hundred miles. Within another twenty miles you reach the incomparable estuary, the Firth of Clyde. There the river becomes a miniature sea, with great fiords stretching into awesome mountains, with delectable islands, with long, sandy shores, and with 1,240 square miles of salt water.

Many a sea-captain or ship's engineer will tell you that, though they have sailed the Seven Seas (and a few extra ones), they have never looked on such beauty as when they've sailed up the Firth of Clyde, from the volcanic rock of Ailsa Craig to the sheltered waters of the Tail of the Bank. The fact that most of these sea-captains and ship's engineers are Scottish is neither here nor there. If you incline to doubt them, then reflect that the people of Glasgow consider the Firth of Clyde the most beautiful part of the world, and Glaswegians are never wrong!

One odd thing about the Firth of Clyde is that it should really be the Firth of Daer (pronounced " dar "). Twice I have walked every step of the way from the Broomielaw, in the heart of Glasgow, to the source of the River Clyde. And the Clyde starts as the Daer Water—a little spring among the heather, then a burn, then a great dam to provide water for Lanarkshire, and then it is joined by the Powtrail burn at a place called Watermeetings. A number of other burns join it after that, including a wee one

The Clyde near Hyndford Bridge.

called Clyde's Burn, and from that point on it's the River Clyde. This is very unfair to the Daer, but it seems too late to do anything about it.

Still, if justice were done, it would be the River Daer, and we would talk about ships being Daer-built, and Sir Harry Lauder's famous song would have to be rewritten. Instead of

Roamin' in the gloamin'
On the bonny banks o' Clyde,
Roamin' in the gloamin'
Wi' a lassie by your side

it should be

Roamin' in the gloamin'
On the bonny banks o' Daer,
Roamin' in the gloamin'
Wi' a lassie in your car.

Well, the Firth by any other name would smell as sweet, and we'll be satisfied with the Firth of Clyde. And so will you be, if you visit us and take the advice I give you in this book.

This is not meant to be either a profound or a poetic study of the Firth of Clyde. It's just a popular guide, written by a man who loves this wonderful holiday place and wants to communicate his love and his wonder to you. I have looked for the picturesque and romantic and interesting things " doon the watter." If there's a remarkable legend or a good story to tell, I've told it. And if some of these stories aren't true, they ought to be.

" Doon the watter? " That's the Glaswegian's way of saying " Down the water." A real Glaswegian says it with a glottal stop, so that it sounds something like " Doon the wa'er."

To the Glaswegians going " doon the watter " is going down to the Firth of Clyde. Glasgow is one of the most fortunately placed cities in the world. Going north, the man from Glasgow can be in the Highlands within an hour. Going west, he can be on the Firth of Clyde within an hour. Going south, he can be in the Burns Country within an hour. And going east, he can reach Edinburgh, the capital of Scotland and the home of the famous Festival, in 55 minutes.

In the old days you invariably sailed from the heart of Glasgow, right down the river, to the Firth. You can still do that. But the usual way, nowadays, is to take a train to one of the Clyde ports and sail from there. The whole Firth is laced with steamer routes. Some of our elders say, with tears in their rheumy eyes, that the Clyde fleet isn't what it used to be. Well, of course it isn't. In the days of cheap coal and low wages it was easy to run a steamer on the Clyde. These were the days, too, of unlimited competition—the days when three or four steamers would race for a pier which could take only one at a time. Our elders' rheumy eyes light up when they talk about the steamer racing, but they seem to have forgotten that boilers burst, people were killed, piers were damaged and captains lost their command in the racing days.

The Clyde fleet today belongs mainly to British Railways, though under the good old name of the Caledonian Steam Packet Company. The firm of MacBrayne's run a steamer service from Gourock to Loch Fyne, and there are one or two privately owned ferries. The main fleet includes paddle steamers, turbine steamers, motor vessels and car ferries. These car ferries (not approved of by our elders) are in the process of revolutionising Clyde travel. They are tremendously popular with motorists. If you look at the map, you'll see why.

Until the introduction of the car ferry, only a few cars could be shipped to the islands in the Firth—Bute, the Big Cumbrae and Arran. And, while it is possible to reach Dunoon and the Cowal coast by road, it is a long and roundabout journey. Now the car ferry takes the automobiles into its capacious maw at Gourock, transports them across the Firth, and decants them at Dunoon. The whole Firth of Clyde is opened up to motorists in a way that it never was before.

Apart from the ferry routes, there are the excursions in the summer, and in 1958 there were 17 ships (including

MacBrayne's "St. Columba") lacing the Firth of Clyde from the end of May to the end of September. They ranged in age from the " Duchess of Montrose," a turbine steamer built in 1930 by Denny's of Dumbarton, to the " Glen Sannox," the 1,000 ton car ferry built in 1957 at Troon. And they ranged in size from the same " Glen Sannox " to the little 39 ton motor vessels, " Ashton " and " Leven," both built by Denny's in 1938.

There are 19 steamer captains employed by the Caledonian Steam Packet Company, and I'm proud to say that I have met them all. They're a fine lot. Some of them are deep sea sailors, who have settled down now in the Firth of Clyde (where, by the way, you can get rough seas too in the winter time). They've had all kinds of adventures, though they are not given to talking about themselves much. " Oh, yes," one of them admits shyly, " I took the ' Marmion ' into Dunkirk four times." Remembering how the British Army were rescued, I ask excitedly, " And what happened ? " " Oh, we got back all right," he says.

One Clyde steamer captain trawled for mines in the canals of Venice. Another served with the Hudson's Bay Company in the far north. All had war experiences, several

' Glen Sannox. *British Railways.*

of them in both wars. Some of them took their steamers to war and saw them sink. Nine ships have been built since the Second World War ended.

Now, before we start our voyage down the Firth of Clyde, may I give you some advice?

First of all, however you are going to travel—by steamer all the way, by train and steamer, by car and steamer—check your journey first. If you are in Glasgow, any of the four main railway stations will be able to give you full particulars of all trains and steamer sailings. Or you can go to the Glasgow Corporation Information Kiosk in St. Enoch Square where you'll get not only information but even a complete itinerary if you want one. There are also regular advertisements in the newspapers, and the Glasgow man's " Bible "—" Murray's Diary." It's really " Murray's Time-Table " and costs sixpence (but you'd better check that too!). It is published every month and gives the times of all the trains from Glasgow and the steamers on the Clyde, the length of the journey and what it will cost.

I mention Glasgow first, because it's the natural place to start from. The whole pattern of the Firth of Clyde sailings is based on Glasgow. But, of course, you could make Edinburgh your jumping-off place if you don't object to adding an hour to your journey in each direction. Another, and very popular, way to cover the Clyde is to stay in one of the coast resorts. The principal places on the Firth are all well served for steamers in the summer, and you could make your base Gourock, or Helensburgh (travelling from Craigendoran pier), or Dunoon, or Wemyss Bay (which includes Skelmorlie), or Rothesay.

Piers on the Firth of Clyde, by the way, are mostly in the strictly functional class. There isn't one that even remotely resembles the piers at Blackpool or Brighton. But I must give you a word of warning here. Some visitors come to the Clyde with maps, and they have worked out their holiday travels according to the piers shown on these maps. Well, the maps are correct. There *is* a pier (or sometimes just part of a pier) at every point where it's marked on the map, but that doesn't necessarily mean that the steamers call there. It costs so much to run a steamer nowadays that, where one pier can do the work of two or three—and linking with buses makes this possible—the authorities have concentrated on that pier.

How about weather? Well, the weather is just about the average for Britain. The best months are usually May, June and September, and October can be wonderful too. Some cynics describe July and August as the " monsoon period " on the Clyde but, like so many other cynical remarks, that's not true. Generally speaking, temperatures are equable, and you get neither very cold winters nor very warm summers. It doesn't rain nearly as much as the natives would have you believe. But a typical joke on the Firth is the one told of the Holy Loch—" If you cannot see across the loch," says the local wit, " it's raining. And if you *can* see across the loch, it's going to rain!"

For clothing you are advised to be prepared for rain. And remember, too, that it is sometimes colder when you are travelling aboard a ship than it is on land. This warning, of course, is for those who are determined to stay on deck. Every Clyde steamer has plenty of inside accommodation.

I trust I'm not frightening you by all this. Some visitors to Scotland have most peculiar ideas about our weather. I remember a film company which sent a unit from London to the Firth of Clyde in the month of April to do some scenic background shots for a picture. These brave chaps equipped themselves with fur coats, snow-shoes and all the things they knew they'd need in what to them was the Far North. Their background material was to last something less than two minutes on the screen, but the unit manager was told that he'd have three weeks to shoot it—and, if the weather was as bad as it usually was in Scotland (film director speaking), he could take another three weeks.

Well, when the film unit got to the Firth of Clyde they found themselves in a minor heat wave. They completed all their shooting in three days.

The beach at Prestwick.

Now as to eating, drinking, and places to stay. I was looking over a guide book to Scotland published just ten years ago and was entranced to come across this jewel—" Restaurants in the usual sense of the word are found only in Edinburgh, Glasgow, Dundee and Aberdeen." No wonder there are people in London who still think that Scotland is a country consisting almost entirely of bens and glens, where the wild haggis roams free.

The main resorts of the Firth of Clyde have plenty of hotels, boarding houses (which often call themselves " private " hotels), restaurants, tea rooms, cafés and pubs. Indeed, in a place like Largs there is an embarrassment of riches. As you might expect, however, in some of these resorts and in practically all the smaller places, the trade is seasonal and hotels and restaurants close for the winter.

Hotels in Scotland have a good reputation, and there are actually some places where the guests have been known to complain of having too much food! The one thing which you may have to get accustomed to is the Scottish " high tea." Most hotels of any pretensions serve dinner, but the smaller hotels and the boarding houses serve high tea at about six each evening. It consists normally of a hot dish, which may be anything from fish to a grilled steak, accompanied by tea, bannocks, and toast, and followed by more tea, scones, cakes and biscuits. It can be a very good meal indeed, though there are Scots who say that it's much better if you have a glass of whisky as an aperitif.

This brings me to drinking, and I have to confess that the licensing laws on the Firth of Clyde are just as archaic as they are in the rest of Scotland. Pubs and bars close early, even by English standards. The licensing hours vary from place to place. If you are staying in a licensed hotel, of course, you have no problem. You are a guest and may have a drink any time you like—in theory, at least. Then there is the " bona-fide traveller " nonsense.

This applies to Sundays when, by law, all pubs are closed. But hotels with a seven-day licence may remain open to furnish drink to " bona-fide travellers." This means that, if you are a genuine traveller, you can stop at any hotel and have " reasonable refreshment," after signing the travellers' register. But who's to know who is a genuine traveller, and who's to decide what a reasonable refreshment is? In some places it is held that travelling three miles is enough to qualify you for a Sunday drink. But then you are not supposed to be travelling merely for the sake of getting a drink!

On the Isle of Arran, for example, the three main resorts on the east coast—Brodick, Lamlash and Whiting Bay—seem to have been thoughtfully placed just far enough from each other as to qualify a man for a reasonable refreshment on the Sabbath. But I know of a traveller who went from Lamlash to Brodick, signed the book in a hotel there and was reasonably consuming his refreshment when a policeman walked in. He asked where this traveller was going and the traveller replied that he was going back to Lamlash. The policeman pointed out to the traveller that this looked as though he had just done the journey for the drink. So the traveller replied, " In that case, I'll go on to Corrie."

Corrie is the next village north of Brodick, and the traveller travelled the six miles to the hotel there, signed the book, and had another reasonable refreshment. Doubtless if the policeman had followed him to Corrie, the traveller would have gone over the hill to Lochranza and had yet another reasonable refreshment in the hotel there.

You'll be thinking we are very uncivilised in Scotland. Well, we do have some peculiar customs but, after all, a visitor doesn't want to see and do just the same things as he sees and does at home.

You will find the Firth of Clyde a simple and straightforward place on the whole. Its main attraction is the wonderful scenery, though there are plenty of facilities for almost every sport and game you can mention. In particular, it's wonderful for golf, yachting, fishing, walking and climbing. It's also good for boating, bathing, water ski-ing, tennis, bowling, and even (in one place) ice-skating.

In the evening in the resorts of any size there are cinemas and a summer show, notable for the appearance of a special kind of comedian called a " Scotch comic." Most Scotch comics come from Glasgow, and unkind people say that that's because you couldn't live in Glasgow if you didn't see the funny side of things. Also in the evening there are dances, and this applies to all sorts and shapes of resorts on the Clyde. Even the smallest clachan has a hall of some kind and, at the height of the holiday season, the dancing seems never to stop.

But, after all, it's the Firth itself that is the great attraction for visitors. I started with Sir Harry Lauder and I'll finish this " Welcome to the Clyde " with Sir Harry again.

For some years he lived at Dunoon, on the Cowal coast of the Clyde. When he wrote his autobiography, *Roamin' in the Gloamin'*, Lauder said this:—

" I wish all my readers could see the scene upon which I gazed with an almost holy rapture a few minutes ago. I had gone upstairs and strolled through an open window on to the balcony which overlooks the water. It is a lovely evening in early June, the close of a day perfectly heavenly on Clydeside. The sun is going down in a glory of crimson and gold, and the spreading sweeps of the Firth of Clyde are bathed in the splendour of its slow-fading beams. There is not a ripple on the waters, for the wind has died down with the turn of the tide, leaving all the white-sailed yachts like tiny fairy ships dotted between the Cumbraes and Craigendoran, and from my own bit of foreshore to the coasts of Renfrew and Ayr opposite . . . Oh, but it's a braw, braw scene; the wide world over which I have wandered for twenty years can offer me none so fair or heartwarming."

So now we'll go sailing down the busy river into the romantic Firth.

E

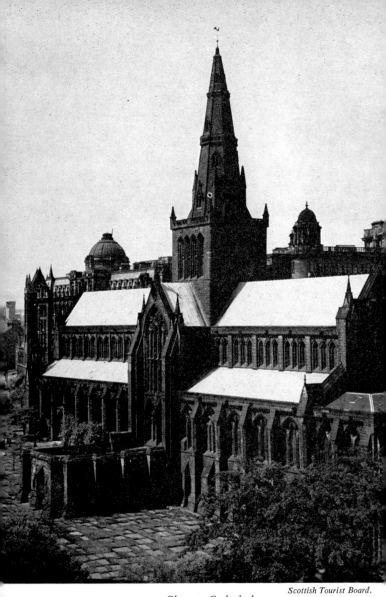

Glasgow Cathedral.

CHAPTER TWO

GLASGOW MADE THE CLYDE

THERE are a number of clichés about the Clyde, and I shall repeat them all in this book. A cliché becomes a cliché because it's an apt way of saying something, and when everybody says the same thing, it becomes boring. But the Clyde clichés are known only to the Clydesiders, and this is a book for visitors.

The first cliché is, " Glasgow made the Clyde, and the Clyde made Glasgow." This is certainly true. About 200 years ago a boy could wade across the river at the very spot where the steamer now waits to take you doon the watter. The Clyde was more famous for salmon than for anything else. Indeed, there's a famous story that apprentices in Glasgow had a clause in their indentures preventing them from being fed with salmon more than twice or thrice a week. So far, however, nobody has been able to produce even a single copy of an indenture with a clause like this.

The ancient Govan Weavers guild always had salmon, boiled eggs and " white wine " for their annual dinner. (The " white wine " is whisky, of course.) They still hold their annual dinner, but now it's just boiled eggs and whisky. The last time salmon were seen in the river in any numbers was at Govan in 1875.

The merchants of Glasgow realised as far back as 1566 that they could improve trade if they could deepen their river. But it wasn't till after the Act of Union between Scotland and England in 1707 that matters became desperate for the Glasgow merchants. They saw all the trade going through Greenock, and they tried to beat Greenock by building their own Port Glasgow next door. But in 1768 an engineer from Chester, John Golborne, produced a scheme for deepening the Clyde. He built breakwaters, walls and jetties, deepened a ford near Dumbarton, dredged the river, and removed an island or two. When he finished the job in 1775 he'd deepened the Clyde even more than he said he would, so the Glasgow magistrates paid him an extra £1,500 on the contract price and gave him a silver cup.

Ever since then the Clyde Navigation Trust have been dredging and deepening, and now the river is from 24 to 30 feet deeper than it was originally. Glasgow has really made the Clyde into a big canal—except, of course, that it's tidal.

I've said all this to impress you, because you probably won't be impressed when first you see the River Clyde in the middle of Glasgow. It doesn't look very wide and it doesn't look over-clean, though it has lost the smell that

Glasgow and the River Clyde.

Scottish Tourist Board.

worried our Victorian ancestors. If you stand on the King George V Bridge and look down the river, you'll maybe find it difficult to believe that on this drumly water have been launched the world's biggest ships and that it becomes one of the world's most beautiful estuaries. On your right is the Broomielaw, once described to me by a sea captain as the second most desperate waterfront in the world. That's a wild exaggeration, but all the same, if you want to explore the Broomielaw, you're better to do it by day.

On your left is Bridge Wharf, where the doon the watter steamer leaves from. It may be the " Queen Mary II," which is really the first " Queen Mary." But when the 81,235-ton Cunarder was launched at Clydebank, the 918-ton turbine steamer relinquished her right to the name of the new " Queen Mary." A brass plate aboard the steamer mentions the thanks of the Cunard Company for this graceful act.

We board the steamer and look to the north to see the headquarters of the Clyde Navigation Trust, which administers the Port of Glasgow. You can pick it out from the other buildings because of its dome and the sculpture which includes a bull, horses, Neptune and sea horses. The interior of this building is as palatial as the City Chambers in George Square. The Clyde Trust controls six tidal docks and $12\frac{1}{2}$ miles of quays, 148 out of the 184 cranes, 71 acres of sheds, $58\frac{1}{2}$ miles of railways, six graving docks, accommodation for 3,500 cattle and for 54,000 tons of grain. It's true that Glasgow has poured millions of pounds into the Clyde, and has got tens of millions back.

The building with the round tower, near the Clyde Trust headquarters, is the Sailors' Home.

The steamer gives a warning hoot and we start our sail. Right in front of us the first of the Clyde ferries cuts across the river. There are 11 of these ferries and five of them carry vehicles as well as passengers. Within the Glasgow area they are free, but you pay to cross Renfrew and Erskine ferries. There were before the war little " Cluthas " (" Clutha " is the poetic name for the Clyde) which took you down the river, but they went to the war and never came back. In Victorian days the " Cluthas " were penny steamers which sailed from quay to quay. But nowadays your only way of seeing the river activities (apart from this sail) is to travel by ferry. Some adventurous souls " lace the river " by crossing on the first ferry, walking to the second and crossing there, walking to the third, and so on. This is fairly arduous and the scenery on land is somewhat drab.

On the north side we see some of the Burns-Laird steamers which ply to Ireland. On the south there is a drawbridge spanning the entrance to Kingston Dock. This is the first Glasgow wet dock, opened in 1867. Today only small ships, sailing vessels and puffers use Kingston Dock. You will see plenty of puffers on the river and the Firth. They were immortalised by Neil Munro in *Para Handy* and by the film, " The Maggie." They carry coal and other cargoes from Glasgow to ports all up and down the western seaboard of Scotland.

The important-looking building you see behind Kingston Dock belongs to the Scottish Co-operative Wholesale Society. It looks important because it was one of the designs submitted for the City Chambers in Glasgow. This design gained second prize and you can compare it with the design which won.

Next on the north side come the quays where new vessels are fitted out, and over on the south the huge ore-discharging plant at General Terminus Quay. Iron ore is brought in here, discharged, and loaded into trains for the Lanarkshire iron and steel works. You'll notice that the men working on the unloading all wear steel helmets. We'll be seeing the shipbuilding yards soon, and there's an old story that the foremen in these yards always wore steel-lined bowler hats— just in case some humorous workman above them dropped a bit of his work.

On the north is the great bulk of the 175-ton fitting-out electric crane, the biggest on the Clyde. Away up on Gilmorehill behind the crane is Glasgow University. Some

critics refer to it contemptuously as "wedding-cake" architecture. It was designed by Sir George Gilbert Scott and opened in 1870. The University was founded in 1451 in the High Street of Glasgow. The two Oriental-looking towers to the east are a theological college and a kirk.

Now we come to Queen's Dock on the north and Princes Dock on the south and by this time you should be accustomed to seeing ships from all parts of the world. Just past the docks on the north is Yorkhill Quay where Anchor liners dock from America and India. The big red buildings on the hill behind are the Royal Sick Children's Hospital.

And now you hear the start of the Clyde symphony—described by a Glasgow man as "a helluva bashin' noise." We are at the beginning of the long line of shipyards. About one-third of all the shipbuilding in Britain is done here—indeed, more ships are built here than in any other one place in the entire world. During the Second World War the Clyde built nearly 2,000 ships, repaired over 23,000, and converted hundreds of others. That's to say they built or repaired at least 13 ships a day for five years. And they are still building the biggest and the best ships in the world here.

By the way, when you are passing the shipyards, it's the custom to wave from the steamer to the men perched high among the forest of tree stems and the dark red masses of steel. You can depend on it that they'll wave back.

The first shipbuilding yard we come to is Harland and Wolff's on the south side. They have seven berths and they build tankers and cargo vessels up to 750 feet. When all out they can build 75,000 tons of shipping in a year.

On the north side the River Kelvin joins the Clyde—on the Kelvin's banks are the Glasgow University, the Art Galleries (finest municipal collection in Britain), and Kelvingrove Park, but all you can see from here is the Pointhouse Shipyard belonging to A. and J. Inglis. They specialise in train ferries, coasters and tugs, and also make whalers and fishery research vessels.

Next to Pointhouse are Henderson's ship repair yard and then the great Meadowside Granary. Opposite the Granary is Fairfield yard, where more than 10,000 men will be employed if the orders are good. Fairfield build liners and warships, up to a length of 1,000 feet. They have six berths, and among the famous ships they have made are the battleship " Howe," the aircraft carrier " Bellona," and the liners " Transylvania " and " Letitia."

The district behind these two great yards on the south (Harland and Wolff's and Fairfield) is Govan, and you'll have noted Govan Pier, once quite a centre of Clyde travel, but no longer used by the river steamers. The Burgh of Govan is, officially, inside Glasgow, but the inhabitants do not regard themselves as Glaswegians. I have already mentioned the Govan Weavers' annual supper of boiled eggs and whisky (which I have attended and enjoyed), and the Govan Old Fair is held on the same evening. Govan Parish Church is well worth a visit, for the finest collection

of Druidical and early Christian monuments in Scotland is to be seen there.

Back on the north side we see Merklands lairage, where the cattle come in from Ireland, and across the river is Stephen's Linthouse shipyard.   Stephen's can turn out 50,000 tons a year of liners, warships, cargo boats and yachts.   That figure is doubled on the north side by Barclay, Curle's, whose annual output capacity is 100,000 tons. They build passenger and cargo ships and oil tankers. Barclay, Curle's North British Engine Works are next door to their shipyard.   Then comes Connell's yard, which launched many a famous sailing ship, including the " Star of Alaska " and the " Abraham Rydberg."   Nowadays they make cargo boats and transport ferries.   Mechan's yard,

Shipyards of the Clyde.

Aerofilms.

alongside, numbers its launches in hundreds. It specialises in building lifeboats.

Opposite, on the south side of the Clyde, is the King George V Dock, opened by that monarch in 1931. New docks, even bigger, are to be built alongside the King Georve V Dock. The great chimney that you see ahead of you belongs to the Braehead Power Station, and it's said to have the broadest diameter of any chimney in Europe. (Some people say the broadest in the world, but there may be Russian visitors aboard!)

On the north bank there are various factories and works and more shipyards. First, the Blythswood yard, with five berths and an impressive record of tanker construction. Here was built the ship they made a film out of—the " San Demetrio." Yarrow's, next door, build destroyers, gunboats and sloops—and also yachts.

Looking over the land to the south, you can see the tower of Renfrew Town Hall. You'll almost certainly see also an aeroplane taking off or coming in to land at Renfrew Airport, for this airport serves Glasgow and is one of the busiest in Britain. Renfrew doesn't look it, but it is a very ancient town. We are now approaching Renfrew Ferry and on the road up to the town from the south side of the ferry stood the Castle of Renfrew, which saw the start of the Royal House of Stewart, from which our present Queen is descended.

In the 12th century Walter Fitzalan came from Shropshire to the Scottish Court. King Malcolm IV appointed him King's High Steward in 1157 and gave him the lands of Renfrew. The office was a hereditary one and the family called themselves Stewart. In 1314 Walter Stewart was among the bravest of the brave men at the Battle of Bannockburn, and the following year he married Marjory, the daughter of King Robert the Bruce. It was her son who became King of Scotland in 1370 and so started the Stewart line. Marjory was killed by being thrown from her horse while hunting near Renfrew in 1316, and her tomb (or what's said to be her tomb) is in Paisley Abbey, not far away. In the 15th century the heir to the Scottish throne was given the title of Baron Renfrew, and that is one of the titles of the Prince of Wales today.

On the north side of Renfrew Ferry is another great power station, Yoker. And now we are sailing out of Glasgow. It's important to point this out, because people who live in towns contiguous to Glasgow get very annoyed if their place's identity is swallowed up in the great city's. This is especially so of Clydebank, where the " Bankies " are forever contradicting the foul canard that the " Queen Mary " and the " Queen Elizabeth " were built in Glasgow!

But before we come to John Brown's yard, we pass two shipyards on the south side. The first is Simon's and they launched many small war vessels and harbour craft for all parts of the world. Next to them is the Lobnitz yard, making dredgers and tugs, but whose great claim to fame is that they built the prototype Mulberry Harbour, which made the D-Day landings in Normandy such a success in the Second World War.

The big dock on our right, just before John Brown's, is Rothesay Dock. It's not named after the capital of the Isle of Bute, but after King Edward VIII, when he was prince of Wales and Duke of Rothesay. (That's another hereditary title, like Baron Renfrew.)

And now, John Brown's—the great name in Clyde ship-building. Everyone with a camera has a shot at John Brown's. On all sides you hear the two magic names mentioned—" Queen Mary " and " Queen Elizabeth." Yes, this is the place where the two biggest liners in the world (81,235 and 85,000 tons respectively) were launched. Before the " Queen Mary " took the water, a disappointed English shipbuilder, presumably digesting sour grapes, was heard to enquire how it was possible to launch such a leviathan into " that trout stream!" He was referring to the River Clyde, and the fact is that it wouldn't be possible to launch any big ship from John Brown's if it wasn't for the River Cart joining the Clyde just opposite. I saw the " Queen Mary " launched, and it was a triumph of calculation. The ship's stern went up the River Cart and then she came back and was canted round to her berth.

During the Second World War the Nazis mounted their biggest blitz in Scotland on Clydebank. Not one single bomb fell inside John Brown's yard, but only six houses in the whole town were undamaged. A great deal of Clydebank was laid flat, but the workers found new accommodation or lived in the ruins like troglodytes. At any rate, they didn't stop working. They built the biggest ship in the world and took it down the Clyde secretly by night. The "Queen Elizabeth" had no trial runs. She sailed straight across the Atlantic to begin work as a trooper. Could there be a finer testimony to the term "Clydebuilt"?

The world's largest clock face is a suitable accompaniment to the world's largest liner, and it's in Clydebank too. You'll see it from the deck of the steamer. It's part of the Singer Sewing Machine factory, and it is almost 30 feet in diameter.

You wouldn't think, to look at the River Cart and the pastoral land around it, that there's a shipbuilding yard higher up that river. But up near Paisley is Fleming and Ferguson's yard, with eight berths and an output of small passenger ships, tugs and dredgers. Paisley itself is worth a visit. It has a 12th century Abbey, some fine buildings, and is the world centre for thread-making.

However, we sail on, past works, a shipbreaking yard and oil storage tanks on the north bank and agricultural land on the south. The riverside begins to lose its industrial character. We pass Newshot Isle, which is not an island at all but merely a peninsula. There are some elderly wrecks on the shore and the boat-houses at Park Quay are a relic of a scrap depot used in the war.

And we now come by Erskine Ferry to Old Kilpatrick. This ferry connects Dunbartonshire on the north with Renfrewshire on the south. It is the last ferry across the River Clyde. The next ferries we meet will be crossing the Firth.

Erskine House stands in undulating parkland on the south side. It is now the Princess Louise Scottish Hospital for

Limbless Sailors and Soldiers. But it was once the residence of the Blantyre family, and before that Erskine (though not this House) belonged to the Earls of Mar.

Old Kilpatrick, on the other side, lies below the Kilpatrick Hills and is said to be the birthplace of St. Patrick, the patron saint of Ireland. The inhabitants can show you St. Patrick's Well, and they'll tell you the story of how the De'il so beset the Saint that he fled to Ireland. When the De'il saw the holy man escaping, he wrenched a rock from Dumbuck Hill and threw it at him. Fortunately it missed St. Patrick and today it's known as Dumbarton Rock. The Clyde Navigation Trust don't quite agree with this story. They think the De'il threw the stone all right, but it wasn't Dumbarton Rock. They have a stone of their own right in the middle of the river and you'll see it from the steamer deck. It's plainly marked " St. Patrick's Stone Light," because they have a guiding light on top of it.

The Irish, I'm afraid, don't agree that their saint was born in Old Kilpatrick, and this is a downright shame because the Scots have never interfered with any of the Irish legends!

They can't argue, anyway, about the Roman remains that are found hereabouts. Old Kilpatrick was the western end of Antonine's Wall, which ran right across Scotland. It was built to protect the Romans against the fearsome Scots. Although the Romans conquered England, they never succeeded in beating the Scots. Indeed, the only people who have ever really beaten the Scots are the Scots.

On the north side we come to Bowling Harbour, which is the western end of the Forth and Clyde Canal—a waterway which, like Antonine's Wall, crosses Scotland, and keeps remarkably close to the line of the wall. The canal starts at Grangemouth on the Forth and it took 22 years to build. When it was officially opened, on July 28, 1790, a hogshead of water from the Forth was symbolically poured into the Clyde. The canal runs for 35 miles, across the narrow waist of Scotland. Nowadays it is used mainly by yachts and fishing boats, with an occasional midget submarine to keep the excitement going.

Bowling is the meeting place of four different forms of transport. Side by side run the river, the railway, the canal, and the road.

Nestling amidst an army of oil storage tanks is Dunglass Castle, with its obelisk to Henry Bell beside it. Very little remains of the old castle, but part of it is built into a charming mansion house, in which some of the rooms and the furniture were designed by Charles Rennie Mackintosh, the Glasgow architect who became even more famous in Europe than he did in his native land. (The outstanding example of his work in Scotland is the Glasgow School of Art.) The original castle was the seat of the clan of which Sir Ivar Colquhoun of Luss is the present chief.

If you have a map showing a path to Henry Bell's monument, your map is wrong. You can't reach the monument now because it's completely surrounded by the oil depot. Henry Bell is credited with having, through his wee steamer, the "Comet," introduced steam navigation to Europe. (Some have even said he invented the steamboat.) But the experts argue about this. It's certain, however, that he was the pioneer of steamships on the Clyde.

Henry Bell's "Comet" first ran in August, 1812. But ten years before that a stern-wheel steamer, the "Charlotte Dundas," towed two loaded sloops along the Forth and Clyde Canal. It managed $19\frac{1}{2}$ miles in six hours against a strong wind. A number of Clydeside engineers were working on the idea of the steamboat. But in 1811 Henry Bell had the Baths Hotel at Helensburgh and he wanted to encourage trade. So he got his wooden "Comet" (named after a much-talked-of comet in 1811) made by John Wood at Port Glasgow and put in an engine and a boiler made in Glasgow. He thought the novelty of sailing down the Clyde in a steamboat would bring more people to his hotel.

In the *Glasgow Chronicle* on August 14, 1812, he published an advertisement which announced:—" The Steamboat 'Comet.' Between Glasgow, Greenock and Helensburgh. For passengers only.

"The subscriber, at much expense, having fitted up a handsome vessel to ply upon the River Clyde from Glasgow, to sail by the power of air, wind, and steam, intends that the vessel shall leave the Broomielaw on Tuesdays, Thursdays and Saturdays about mid-day, or such an hour thereafter as may answer for the state of the tide, and to leave Greenock on Mondays, Wednesdays and Fridays in the morning to suit the tide.

"The elegance, safety, comfort and speed of this vessel require only to be seen to meet the approbation of the public, and the proprietor is determined to do everything in his power to merit general support."

Henry went on to say that the best cabin would be four bob a nob, and the second class three shillings. Her captain was a Helensburgh schoolmaster, William Mackenzie, and she had a crew of eight, including a piper.

According to Captain James Williamson, in his famous (and now difficult to get) book, *The Clyde Passenger Steamer*, "She was the first vessel moved by steam which successfully carried on a regular service in Europe, thirteen years before the opening of the first public railway."

Well, we're still at the obelisk, which was erected in 1839. If you look across the river to the south, you'll see above some trees its twin, over by Bishopton.

Just past Dunglass you can see in the river the remains of the Long Dyke, one of John Golborne's successful ideas to confine the river current and deepen the bed of the Clyde. The dyke runs right down to opposite Dumbarton Rock. The river starts to widen here and you see to the west the Firth itself, with the mountains of Argyll in the background.

On the north there is Dumbuck Hill, with a great quarry eating into it. Among the buildings on the shore is the original factory of Kosmoid, Ltd., one of the great scandals of the West of Scotland in Victorian days. A Glasgow doctor, James Shiels, claimed to be able to make gold from lead and do other wonderful transmutations. He convinced some of the leading scientists, industrialists and business men of the day and they put up the money for

Kosmoid. Dr. Shiels also took in Dumbarton Town Council, and proposed that a new town should be built in this area with houses right on the top of Dumbuck Hill. But the bubble burst and Dr. Shiels disappeared.

And now we come to Dumbarton Rock, which looks from the west rather like the Rock of Gibraltar on a small scale. Dumbarton Rock is 260 feet high and a mile in circumference. It's said to have been occupied by the Romans, but Dumbarton Castle goes back only to the Scottish wars of independence in the 13th and 14th centuries. Besides being known to the Romans and the Caledonians, Dumbarton Rock is supposed to have been the site of some of the adventures of King Arthur and the Knights of the Round Table. The Vikings attacked it. Sir John Menteith, the traitor who betrayed Sir William Wallace to the English, was governor of Dumbarton Castle, and you can see his face and Wallace's on either side of a gateway. You can tell which is Menteith because he has a finger in his cheek, the sign of a traitor. Wallace was kept in Dumbarton Castle until it was time to take him to London for his " trial " and execution.

Mary, Queen of Scots, sailed from Dumbarton Rock when she was six. She was being taken to France for her own safety. She returned to Scotland and started her unhappy reign. In 1571 she was fighting for her kingdom and she had only two castles left in the hands of her supporters, Edinburgh and Dumbarton. She was making for Dumbarton Castle when she was defeated at the Battle of Langside (now part of Glasgow), but even if she had reached it, she'd have found it already in the hands of her enemies.

The daring Captain Crawford of Jordanhill led an expedition by night against the castle. A guide, one of the soldiers of the castle whose wife had been whipped by order of the Governor for thieving, showed them the way up the rock face. They went up using ladders and scaling hooks. Near the top one of the soldiers took an epileptic fit. His hands could not be removed from the rungs, so Captain

Crawford bound him to the ladder and turned it the other way round so that the invaders could keep climbing. The attack was completely successful.

Cromwell's troops occupied Dumbarton Castle, and much later, in 1745, some of Bonnie Prince Charlie's friends were imprisoned there. Queen Victoria once held a court on the Rock, and the British Royal family have been visiting it ever since. It's well worth a visit if you don't mind heights. The view from the higher of the two peaks (known as Wallace's Seat) is magnificent.

The River Leven runs round the Rock to join the Clyde. It has come from Loch Lomond only a few miles away. Behind the Rock you see Dumbarton. The shipyard there is a famous one—Denny's. If you are travelling aboard the " Queen Mary II " you'll be interested to know that she was built there. The huge red building is Hiram Walker's distillery, the second largest Scotch whisky distillery in the world. (Perhaps I should point out, though, that Scotch whisky can be made only in Scotland.) Just behind the distillery you'll see on a clear day the famous Ben Lomond.

Dumbarton is a corruption of " Dun Breaton," the fort of the Britons. While the town is called Dumbarton, the county is called Dunbartonshire. Alexander II made Dumbarton a Royal Burgh in 1222. Some people called it " the town that missed its chance," because it could have been the port of Glasgow. In 1668 Glasgow suggested this to the Dumbarton magistrates, but they declined because they feared " the influx of mariners should raise the price of butter and eggs to the townsmen." However, as Glasgow made Port Glasgow and then gave it up when the Clyde was deepened up to the Broomielaw, maybe Dumbarton didn't miss much of a chance after all.

There is not much to be seen of history in Dumbarton. The old town house of the Earls of Glencairn stands in the main street, and the broken arch of the Collegiate Church founded in 1450 is near the Burgh Hall. Admirers of the works of A. J. Cronin, the novelist, will be interested in Dumbarton because it's the scene of his first novel,

Hatter's Castle. Cronin was born at Cardross, not far from Dumbarton. The "Levenford" of *Hatter's Castle* is Dumbarton, and the "Garshake" is Cardross itself.

The steamer route now tends to the south shore of the Clyde. On the Dumbarton side the large building standing in grounds surrounded by the living-boxes of Council housing is Keil School, a public school for boys from the Highlands and specialising in agricultural subjects.

On the south side you see the village of Langbank and the mansion on the hill farther on is Finlayston House, another seat of the Earls of Glencairn. In 1556 the Earl of Glencairn was the first Scottish noble to become a Protestant, and John Knox preached at Finlayston House and dispensed Communion there.

The stumps of wood that you see sticking out of the water on the south bank are relics of the days when Port Glasgow did a big timber business with America. These posts were built round the timber ponds.

Just before we sail past Port Glasgow, let's turn again to the north. Not far from Dumbarton was Cardross Castle, where Robert the Bruce died in 1329. He was interested in boat building in his latter years and it's not too fanciful to say that he laid the foundations of a Scottish navy in the little ships he had built at Dumbarton.

Nothing remains of Cardross Castle, but it stood on a piece of ground now called Castlehill, which was given to the National Trust for Scotland by that great writer, horseman and Scottish patriot, Robert Cunninghame Graham. A cairn 12 feet high is a memorial to " Don Roberto," and it includes a profile of Cunninghame Graham, the head of his horse, which he rode for 20 years without a fall, and stone from Argentine and Uruguay sent by the author's admirers in South America.

You can see the village of Cardross, a bonny wee place, on the shore, and then the wooded promontory of Ardmore, with its mansion house.

All the good scenery at this point is on the north. To the

Overleaf—Dumbarton Rock

south is drab Port Glasgow, built up the side of a steep hill. The views *from* Port Glasgow are wonderful. The view *of* Port Glasgow is not so good. In the 17th century the Glasgow merchants were jealous of Greenock's harbour business. As I've said, they tried to get Dumbarton to become the port of Glasgow. When Dumbarton refused, the Glasgow men decided to build their own port. So in 1668 they founded Port Glasgow, a mere three miles from Greenock. In 1762 the first graving-dock on the Clyde was built here. Port Glasgow flourished until John Golborne deepened the river. Then, in 1806, the " Harmony " of Liverpool, a brig of 120 tons, sailed right up from the Firth to Glasgow itself, and Port Glasgow was no longer the port of Glasgow.

Now Port Glasgow is an industrial town and looks it. The first yard you see belongs to Smith and Houston, the shipbreakers, and at least one example of their work will almost certainly be lying there for you to see. Then comes Lamont's shipyard, and then, huddling in the middle of all this industry, Newark Castle. This castle is open to the public, if you can find it when you're in Port Glasgow! It is an old stronghold of the Maxwell family, and they lived there until the beginning of the 18th century. It was a Sir Patrick Maxwell who sold the 22 acres of land to the Glasgow merchants to establish their port in 1668.

Penning the castle in on the east is Ferguson Brothers' shipyard. Then comes the two harbours of Port Glasgow. The big red building at the back belongs to Gourock Ropeworks, a firm which started in Gourock all right, but flitted to Port Glasgow. Besides making miles and miles of ropes for all purposes (including the ropes for both the " Queen Mary " and the " Queen Elizabeth "), they have built several of the big tops for Bertram Mills' Circus.

On the waterfront we come now to one of the two yards, the East, owned by Lithgows, a very famous name among Clyde shipbuilders. Their yards are divided by William Hamilton's shipyard, and the Lithgow establishment on the other side is Kingston Yard.

Well, we're almost at Greenock now. From the steamer deck you can't tell where Port Glasgow ends and Greenock begins. But now we are at the Tail of the Bank, the end of the sand bank which runs from Dumbarton right down to Greenock. We have sailed down the river and now we see the wide sweep of the Firth of Clyde.

CHAPTER THREE

THE PORTS OF THE CLYDE

THERE are a score of places on the Firth of Clyde which might call themselves ports, but I am going to deal in this chapter with just three of them—Craigendoran, Gourock and Wemyss Bay. From these three ports the regular services go to almost everywhere on the Firth, and cruising steamers *do* go everywhere.

I'll deal with Craigendoran first, since it's the " sport " of the ports—the only one on the north bank of the Clyde. Craigendoran (the name comes from the Gaelic and means " The rock of the otter ") is reached by road from Cardross and by rail from Edinburgh. Before British Railways took over, it was the pier for the London and North Eastern Railway, and it is the way that you get to the Firth if you come direct from the Capital of Scotland.

Craigendoran is also the starting point of the West Highland Railway, one of the finest (some say *the* finest) scenic runs in the whole railway system of Britain. It goes up to Fort William and part of the run is along the eastern bank of Loch Long, one of the fiords of the Firth.

It's the pier if you are staying in Helensburgh, for the pier there is not used now. Craigendoran is really a suburb of Helensburgh, which you can read about in my next chapter. The paddlers, " Jeanie Deans " and " Talisman," leave from Craigendoran pier, which somehow looks quite different from any other pier on the Clyde.

We cross the Firth by the Tail of the Bank to Greenock. The Tail of the Bank is a famous anchorage, and during the war gigantic fleets mustered here. You are almost certain to see some big ships at anchor, for this is where the transatlantic liners stop, both to embark and disembark passengers. Inward bound ships also anchor here to await a suitable tide.

Ashore I left you just where Port Glasgow turns into Greenock, and if you are sailing down the Clyde from Glasgow you now pass the last group of shipyards that make the 22 great Clyde yards. If you are sailing past them just after noon, don't imagine that the complete silence means a strike. It happens to be dinner time, and the workers melt away like snow off a dyke.

We pass the Great Harbour of Greenock and the James Watt Dock and come to Garvel Shipyard (George Brown's). This name will ring a bell with you if you have read the novels of George Blake, the chronicler of the Clyde. He wrote *The Shipbuilders*, *The Constant Star*, *The Westering Sun*, and many others. Most of these novels are placed in a town which Mr. Blake calls " Garvel," but which bears a strong resemblance to his native place, Greenock.

After Garvel Shipyard comes the Greenock Dockyard Company, and then the oldest shipbuilding firm in the world, Scott's. It was established in 1771 and the first vessels launched were fishing boats. It's still a family concern. Scott's is not only the first but also the last shipbuilding yard on the Clyde. After it we pass various harbours and the fine front of the Custom House and come to Princes Pier, which once was an important part of the Clyde steamer set-up. Steamers no longer call there, but tenders bring liner passengers ashore at Prince's Pier.

Greenock looks somewhat more impressive from the water than it does when you are in the town. The tall, Italianate tower is part of Greenock Town Hall. From the water you can't see the blitzed bits of the town. A distillery on the hill was hit in one of the Second World War raids and a river of flaming whisky ran down the slope into the town.

This is an industrial town—" ships and sugar " are the main industries—and it looks it, until you come to the space and dignity of Greenock's West End. Nevertheless it's a popular town with many sailors and service men from all over the world. The great convoys came into the Tail of the Bank and troops from America, Canada and many other places landed at Princes Pier to set foot for the first time in Europe. Many Americans and Canadians have since returned to the town on holiday. As in the case of Port Glasgow, the views *from* Greenock are wonderful, for the Clyde here is four miles wide over to Helensburgh. The sea and mountain scenery is superb.

Originally Greenock was a tiny fishing village. Then the laird, Sir John Schaw, and some supporters, got Greenock made a burgh in 1707. The port was established, industry grew, and eventually Greenock was so big and prosperous that the Greenockians even promoted a bill to establish a university in the town. It failed. And Greenock itself came to something of a halt when Glasgow deepened the Clyde and brought the ships up past the Tail of the Bank.

Greenock was the birthplace of the great inventor, James Watt; also of the poet, John Davidson, and of the pirate, Captain Kidd. John Galt, the novelist and Empire builder, lived and died in the town, although he was born in Irvine. Hamish MacCunn, composer of the popular overture, " The Land of the Mountain and the Flood," was born in Greenock. So was Jean Adams, who is supposed to have written one of the best Scottish songs, " There's nae luck aboot the hoose," though there's another claimant to the authorship.

For Burns enthusiasts Greenock is famous as the place where Highland Mary (born across the Firth at Dunoon) is buried. She was originally interred in the West Kirk burying ground, but it was taken over for a shipyard extension, and she was reburied in the new Greenock Cemetery.

Various Gaelic scholars give different origins of the name Greenock. According to one school, it comes from " grian," the sun, and " cnoc," a hill, so it means " the sunny hill." Others say it's from " grian-aig," a sunny bay. If either of these is correct, the weather must have changed radically since Greenock got its name, for it's famous as the wettest place on the whole of the Clyde—indeed, the West of Scotland.

We sail on from Princes Pier, by Fort Matilda, the Admiralty torpedo works, and across Cardwell Bay to Gourock pier. As the steamer crosses the bay, look back at the Lyle Hill behind Greenock and you'll see the Cross of Lorraine. It's the monument to the men of the Free French naval forces who sailed from the Clyde and died in action in the Second World War.

Above Gourock is Tower Hill, with an elderly watch-tower (used during the war as an observers' spotting post) on the top of it. All around here you see activity on the waters. Ships are sailing up and down the Clyde. Steamers and ferries are criss-crossing the Firth. The busy wee boats of the Clyde Pilotage are taking pilots out from Gourock to

The Free French Memorial at Gourock.
Scottish Tourist Board.

board incoming ships or bringing them back from outgoing
ships. And almost certainly steamers are manoeuvring at
Gourock pier, for this is the most important of all the
steamer centres.

Although you will not have noticed any break in building
from Port Glasgow, through Greenock, to Gourock, you
will see now that Gourock looks very different from the
two industrial towns. An ecstatic publicity man once
named Gourock " the Glad Eye of the Clyde," but that's
rather overstating it. It is the first holiday resort we've
touched at, and has all the appurtenances, including a
bathing pool, a summer theatre, promenades, and so on.
It is, as I have suggested, a good place to make your headquarters if you want to spend a week or so sailing on the
Firth.

Gourock is built round Kempock Point and not far from
the pier, although you can't see it from either the pier or the
steamer, is the Kempock Stone, known locally as " Granny
Kempock." It is all that remains of an altar to Baal in
Druidical times, and today it is surrounded by superstition
and tenements. If you want to see it, go up from the pier to
Kempock Street and take the first passage-way to the left.
A lane leads you to the grey stone, about six feet high,
standing within a fence.

Gourock was a port before Greenock was, and the sailors
and fishermen attributed great powers to Granny Kempock.
If you took some earth from around her and used it as
ballast, your ship was safe from evil. Another story is that
sailors would march round Granny Kempock seven times,
carrying baskets of sand and chanting an incantation for a
fair wind and a safe voyage. At a witch trial held in
Gourock in 1662 a teen-age girl named Mary Lamont
confessed that she was a witch and that her coven (twelve
witches and the Devil) had planned to throw Granny
Kempock into the Firth and so destroy the good she did to
sailors. Mary Lamont was burned at the stake.

So far, we have been following in the main the sail from
Bridge Wharf, but now, to reach our third port, Wemyss

Cloch Lighthouse.

Scottish Tourist Board.

Bay, I propose to take you along the shore from Gourock. I have walked all the way from Gourock to the Ayrshire resort of Girvan. This walk took me six days and I'd have enjoyed it much more if the smell of petrol hadn't interfered so much with the ozone.

We go along the Cloch Road, through the Gourock suburb of Ashton, and by the Royal Gourock Yacht Clubhouse, to the Cloch Lighthouse, erected in 1791 and one of the 11 lighthouses on the Firth. From here there is a ferry service to Dunoon, run by private enterprise. The road bears inland at Lunderston Bay and over a hill and down again into the charming village of Inverkip. The name means the mouth of the Kip, the burn which flows into the Clyde at this spot. It was at Inverkip that Mary Lamont, aged 18, confessed that she was a witch before the local minister. She involved several other women, and they also were tortured and burned at the stake.

From the water you see Ardgowan Castle on one side of Inverkip and Castle Wemyss on the other. By road you go inland again, behind Castle Wemyss, to Wemyss (say " Weems ") Bay. Castle Wemyss belonged to the late Lord Inverclyde. Wemyss Bay is the terminus of the railway line from Glasgow, and it's the main port for steamers to Rothesay. The sail to Rothesay takes about half an hour. Wemyss Bay Station has won many prizes for the best-kept railway station in Scotland, and you may well think that it looks more like a conservatory than a station.

Just opposite the station the Kelly Burn runs under the road and into the Clyde. Although Wemyss Bay and Skelmorlie seem one place, they are actually in different counties. The Kelly Burn is the boundary between Renfrewshire on the north and Ayrshire on the south. From the steamer you can't tell the difference, for both villages are built of the local red sandstone, pink and gleaming in the sun. There is a passenger lift up the cliff, so that you may travel up from sea level, instead of taking the steep road

Boarding the car ferry at Wemyss Bay.
Scottish Tourist Board.

to the top. Skelmorlie has a golf course and some enthusiasts assert that it has the best view of any golf course on the Firth of Clyde. You look north to the Cowal shore and the mountains beyond, west to the Isle of Bute, and south to the Isle of Arran and Ailsa Craig.

The wonderful view from Wemyss Bay and Skelmorlie is why these twins are popular with holiday-makers, who can also use Wemyss Bay pier to get around the Firth. To many a ship enthusiast an attraction is one of the two Measured Miles of the Clyde. You can see the posts with their triangular signs just below Skelmorlie Hydro and again a mile down the coast. Most Clyde-built ships are tested on this Measured Mile, but big liners and warships carry out their tests on the Measured Mile off the north of the Isle of Arran.

About the end of the Measured Mile you can see Skelmorlie Castle, and another of the big buildings on this stretch is Knock Castle. And so you arrive at Largs, and another chapter.

CHAPTER FOUR

THE LOST LOCH

L ET'S go right back to the tail of the Bank and across to Craigendoran, for we're going now to investigate the Gare Loch, the first of the lochs of the Firth of Clyde. Gare means short, and this loch is about six miles in length. It was once one of the most beautiful of Clyde lochs and sailing up it to Garelochhead was a quiet delight. Now I call it " the Lost Loch," and that isn't simply because steamers no longer call at its piers. There are cruises up the Gare Loch, but often the only way to see it now is by road.

We start at Helensburgh, the " model town " of the Clyde. It was a wee clachan called Milligs, but the local laird, Sir James Colquhoun, eighth baronet of Colquhoun and Luss and ancestor of the present Sir Ivar Colquhoun, decided to make it a town and call it after his wife, Helen. So Milligs was renamed Helensburgh, and advertisements were put out to attract weavers and bonnet-makers to the place. In 1802, when no weavers or bonnet-makers had shown any signs of arriving, the plan was changed and it was decided to make Helensburgh a residential town built on the lines of the New Town of Edinburgh.

Today if you fly over Helensburgh, you'll see how mathematically it is laid out. The houses are in wide, tree-lined avenues up the side of a hill—indeed, the district is spoken of as " The Hill " with some awe, because the well-to-do live there and have little or no truck with the day trippers who flock down by train and bus from Glasgow in their thousands. The day trippers keep to the promenade and the shore, and the residents keep to The Hill, except for occasional forays to the shopping centre.

Helensburgh.

Scottish Tourist Board.

There is a monument to Henry Bell, the steamboat man, and you can stay at his Baths Hotel, now called the Queen's. Seen from the sea, it's square, white and castellated. Perhaps because he was credited with starting steam navigation in Europe, Henry was made Helensburgh's first Provost (Mayor in England). He is not Helensburgh's only inventor, though. J. L. Baird, the pioneer of television, was born in the manse of Helensburgh. One of his boyhood friends there was that delightful actor, Jack Buchanan. And Deborah Kerr, the film star, spent her youth in Helensburgh.

The Bathing Pool stands by Helensburgh pier, which is no longer used by steamers. Amateurs of murder will be interested in the fact that this pier had a connection with the famous Madeleine Smith case. Madeleine was found " Not Proven " of the murder by poison of her lover, Pierre Emile L'Angelier, in 1857. But on the day the police went to make enquiries at her family home in Blythswood Square, Glasgow, Madeleine disappeared. Her fiancé and her brother went in search of her, and found her aboard a steamer at Helensburgh pier. She was making for the Smith's country home at Rhu, two miles up the Gare Loch from Helensburgh.

We go along the promenade, by the pebbly shore, past Ardencaple Castle to Rhu. Opposite is the promontory of Rosneath, and we'll go right round the Gare Loch to it. Soon you see why I called it the " Lost Loch." This sheltered stretch of water has suffered from two World Wars and the Depression in between. In the First World

War the Admiralty used the Gare Loch as a testing place for submarines. When the Depression came and ships were laid up, they sailed or were towed into the Gare Loch, which became a kind of graveyard of the merchant navy. In those days you could count the rusting ships in the loch by the dozen.

Came the Second World War and the Gare Loch became important in the war effort. The War Office, the Admiralty and the American Services all took their own parts of loch shores. Huge sheds for Coastal Command were built at Rhu, a great port with railway sidings was made at Faslane; over on Rosneath peninsula the Americans used the castle as their headquarters and the ground as a rehearsal base for Combined Operations. Among the American Naval officers there was a certain Robert Montgomery, whom you may have seen on the screen. All up and down the loch the armed forces built barracks and stores.

The war is long over but the Gare Loch has never recovered. As you go up one side and down the other, you keep coming across the remnants of the occupation, and in between are beautiful little places which show you what the Gare Loch was once like.

You walk along a delightful promenade towards Rhu, and then you suddenly come upon these enormous Coastal Command sheds. Past them Rhu is lovely once again. Out in the loch there are " mothballed " warships (" co-cooned " is the proper term) and laid-up merchant ships. But the prospect is more interesting than unpleasing. Rhu is a charming little village, with a kirk on a hill. Henry Bell is buried there, and there are other interesting tombstones.

Rhu means a promontory in the Gaelic. Among the mansions on the hill was the Smith house, where Madeleine met her lover L'Angelier in secret. When she bought arsenic in a shop in Sauchiehall Street, Glasgow, she said it was to kill rats at Rhu. When the doctors conducted a post mortem on L'Angelier they found enough arsenic inside him to kill a hundred rats.

All this part of the country was used by Sir Walter Scott as a background for his novel, *The Heart of Midlothian*. Just past Rhu is a valley to which he gave the name of the Whistler's Glen. But this glen has a spirituous as well as a literary significance. The district was famous for illicit whisky stills and, when King George IV visited this part of Scotland, he said he'd like to taste some of the forbidden whisky. He was a man who liked the good things of life. The Duke of Argyll was asked to provide the water of life, and he was proud when he was able to give the King a bottle of usquebagh from a still in the Whistler's Glen.

You will see many yachts on the water about here, for Rhu is the headquarters of the Royal Northern Yacht Club, the fifth oldest yacht club in the British Isles. Yachting, like golf, is rather more democratic in Scotland than it is in England, and there are several centres on the Firth where you can be taught the art of sailing by experts.

We come into Shandon, where part of the castellated Shandon Hydropathic stands. It was originally the mansion of Robert Napier, the great Clyde engineer and virtual founder of Atlantic travel. Its size and its towers made it the most remarkable building on the whole of the Gare Loch. Until recent years it was kept going as a hydro-hotel. But now it is no more, and only the towers and the battlemented terrace running alongside the road remain.

Once we come round Cairnban Point we see more evidence of what the Second World War did to the loch. Here is Faslane, the huge wartime port, now a naval headquarters and a shipbreakers' yard. You may well see the hulk of some once-famous liner lying by the quays and the rail sidings. The yard covers a great space and on both sides of the road high wire fences have been built, giving nervous pedestrians the feeling that they are in some enormous concentration camp. I speak with feeling, because I walked all the way from Glasgow to Dunoon and I couldn't get through this bit of the road quickly enough. If you're in a car, of course, you're through in no time.

From Faslane a road runs up the hill to the right. It takes you to Glen Fruin, the Glen of Weeping (sometimes called the Glen of Sorrow). Here in 1603 the MacGregors ambushed the Colquhouns, with whom they had been on unfriendly terms for some time. More than a hundred Colquhouns were killed, and even some boys from Dumbarton Grammar School, who had gone along in the hope of seeing a fight! Then the MacGregors attacked the Colquhoun lands round Luss and plundered and pillaged.

The chief of the Colquhouns went to Stirling to lay his case before King James the Sixth (later also King James the First of the United Kingdom). He took with him nearly a hundred widows and they paraded before the King dressed in black and carrying the bloodstained clothes of their dead men. The King was so incensed that he ordered the MacGregors to be outlawed and their name proscribed. So the MacGregors, Rob Roy's clan, became landless and nameless. Their story is told by Scott in *Rob Roy*.

From Faslane we come to Garelochhead which, as its name implies, is the top of the loch. Once again we're in a pleasant little village, and it's possible to forget the mess farther down the water. And yet this quiet wee place had a battle of its own. Maybe the Battle of Garelochhead wasn't as bloody as the battle in Glen Fruin, but it deserves its place in history too.

In early Victorian days the idea of taking a sail on a Sunday was quite unheard of, in middle-class circles anyway. But everyone wasn't middle.class. The hard working people of Glasgow who had only one free day in the week, Sunday, were determined to have as good a time as the middle-class and rich folk who could go doon the watter any day they liked.

On a Sunday towards the end of August, 1853, the steamer " Emperor " came paddling into Garelochhead pier and the passengers and crew found facing them a solid phalanx of police, gillies, and other bodies recruited by Sir James Colquhoun of Luss. Sir James had decided that he wasn't having Sunday trippers anywhere in his domain.

When the " Emperor's " crew cast their ropes ashore, the men on the pier threw them off again. But the Glaswegians aboard the steamer were, as they are today, strong for individual rights. They just jumped on to the pier, secured the ropes themselves, and saw that the passengers were landed.

Sir James's forces reorganised and faced the incomers. But the tourists were not to be denied. Waving sticks and lemonade bottles, they attacked to such purpose that the Colquhoun cohorts were routed. This battle was watched by inhabitants from other Gare Loch villages and they were delighted at the outcome because they were all in favour of the Sunday attackers. Eventually the Sunday sails were forbidden by law, but that's all a hundred years ago and now the pier owners are looking for Sunday visitors!

View of Gare Loch from Whistlefield.

Scottish Tourist Board.

At the top of the Gare Loch the main road goes on to Arrochar and a secondary one turns round the Rosneath peninsula. We take the secondary road, but just before we do, go up the main road about a mile to Whistlefield on the top of the hill. There you will get the sort of view that people dream about. To the south lies the Gare Loch, and from Whistlefield you can't see the signs of " civilisation." To the west lie Loch Long and Loch Goil in majestic grandeur.

Now back to the Gare Loch and down the western side. There is a string of clachans, Mambeg, Rahane and Clynder, and some signs of the " occupation " that's so obvious on the east side. At Clynder there's a hotel and a famous yacht-building yard, McGruer's. We go on to Rosneath and the remains of the Rosneath Castle estate. The now roofless castle was built in 1803, and most of the estate is now a caravan site.

Rosneath was called an island by Sir Walter Scott in *The Heart of Midlothian*, and his general descriptions of the surrounding scenery are not exactly apt. But readers of Scott will recollect that the Duke of Argyll sent for Jeanie Deans to come to Rosneath after her long pilgrimage to London to intercede for her unhappy sister. The Gaelic derivation of Rosneath is " the bare peninsula," but you'll see that it's very well covered indeed.

An old superstition had it that rats could not live on Rosneath soil. A West Indian planter took out a cargo of soil to his plantation because it was infested by rats. But the soil, alas, had no effect, and they say it doesn't kill rats in Rosneath either. It's just as well, though, that the story isn't true or Rosneath peninsula would have disappeared long ago.

As we go over the road by the Gallows Hill, we see two strange-looking leafless trees. They are known locally as Adam and Eve, and are said to be very ancient. Now we come to Kilcreggan, which forms a burgh with its neighbour, Cove. They look like one place, but the Burgh Hall marks the boundary between one village and the other. Kilcreggan has a pier and a private ferry service besides the steamer one. People holiday at Kilcreggan, but it is mainly occupied by West of Scotland business men and their families. The steamer from Gourock to Kilcreggan takes only ten minutes.

There are wonderful views of the Firth from Kilcreggan and Cove. But I shall leave Cove to the next chapter because, although it's all one long line of houses with Kilcreggan, Cove really belongs to Loch Long and the Fiords of the Firth.

CHAPTER FIVE

THE FIORDS OF THE FIRTH

VARIOUS eminent writers have compared the sea lochs of the Firth of Clyde with the fiords of Norway. To me there are only two Clyde lochs that are like Norwegian fiords, and these are Loch Long and Loch Goil.

The summer steamers cruise up both of them—you seldom call at one pier without calling at the other. So this time my description will be from the steamer deck, in the same pattern as I described our voyage from Bridge Wharf to the Tail of the Bank.

The guardian villages of the fiords are Cove on the east and Strone on the west. These places, with their respective twins, Kilcreggan and Blairmore, are typical of the way the Firth of Clyde developed, with wealthy Victorians from Glasgow building summer villas along the shore and on the hill behind.

The castle you see at Cove is known to some as " the largest hen-house in the world." At the time of writing, a local gentleman-farmer is keeping his hens within the castle walls.

Strone is the Gaelic for " nose," and it's a very powerful nose that juts out into the Firth. The hills are steeper on the western shore. The big house you see on the hill above Strone pier is Dunselma, once privately owned and now a Scottish Youth Hostel. It's said that, if you draw a straight line in a south-westerly direction from Strone, it won't touch land until it reaches the coast of Spain.

Around here you may see many small yachts. That's because one of the sailing schools administered by the

National Council for Physical Recreation is based at
Blairmore. Yachting was once a wealthy man's sport on the
Clyde. Now everybody yachts, or maybe I should say
" goes in for sailing."

As the steamer goes north on this 20-mile trip to Arrochar,
at the top of Loch Long, we see the mountains grow
grander and more rugged. They looked even more awe-
inspiring before the Forestry Commission planted the
regiments of trees which now march across their flanks.

Knockderry Castle is on our right. It stands on the
dungeons of an ancient tower, and Scott set the closing
scenes of *The Heart of Midlothian* in it, under the name of
Knock Dunder.

About four miles up we come to Coulport on the right
and Ardentinny on the left. The strange H-shaped erection
near Coulport is an Admiralty ballistic testing station.
Loch Long is used a good deal by the Admiralty.

At Ardentinny on the west you'll pick out the white
hotel and the nice wee kirk alongside it. This is another
place famous among lovers of Sir Harry Lauder's songs.
" Ower the hill," he used to sing,

> Ower the hill tae Ardentinny,
> Just to see ma bonnie Jeanie.

Just behind the clachan you can see Glen Finart and
maybe make out the road " ower the hill." I don't know
whether or not Sir Harry Lauder actually walked ower the
hill tae Ardentinny, but I have. You start from Whistlefield
on Loch Eck and, after a steep climb, you come down a long
slope into the village. The scenery is wonderful, but the day
I did it the rain poured and I saw only ghostly patches of
scenery among the mist. There is a coach tour from
Dunoon which takes you this way, so you can follow the
Lauder route without pain.

Lauder, by the way, was following someone else when
he wrote this song. One of Scotland's poets, Robert
Tannahill, the Paisley weaver who eventually threw himself
into the canal by his native town, visited Ardentinny with a
number of other weavers. In the little hostelry there (now

part of the inn which you can see from the steamer)
Tannahill saw a Highland girl named Jeannie. When he got
back to his loom in Paisley, he wrote one of his best songs,
" The Lass o' Arranteenie," and said of his inamorata—

> Sae sweet amidst her native hills
> Obscurely blooms my Jeannie,
> Mair fair and gay than rosy May,
> The flower o' Arranteenie.

It's sad to relate that Tannahill returned to Ardentinny
to see his Jeannie once again, but the bloom had departed
and she looked just an ordinary girl to him.

At the entrance to the glen is Glenfinart House and by the
roadside there is a well in memory of a former laird's horse.
He rode this horse in battle and, when he left the Army, he
took his horse with him and let it live in equine luxury on
the estate.

The buildings on the north of Finart Bay belong to the
Forestry Commission, and State forests cover all the
mountainside round here.

We sail up Loch Long towards Argyll's Bowling Green,
the great jumble of mountains that separate Loch Goil
from Loch Long. The name is an example of the Highland
sense of humour and can be taken either as a compliment
to, or a slairt at, the ducal family of Campbell. Yes, we are
in the Highlands now. We have been for some time. The
remarkable thing about the Firth of Clyde is that one side
of it is Highland and the other Lowland. The Highland
side is to the north and west. The Lowland to the south
and east. In Scotland the Highland line is not drawn
horizontally across the country, but diagonally, and much
of the Highlands are south of Aberdeen, which is technically
in the Lowlands.

At Bird Point we come to the opening of Loch Goil, and
it might be as well to say once again that this is *not* the
Loch Goil referred to in Thomas Campbell's poem, " Lord
Ullin's Daughter." His Loch Goil is in the Isle of Mull.

Across the water is the village of Portincaple, just below
Whistlefield. This is not the Whistlefield I've already

referred to at Loch Eck on the other side of Glen Finart. It's the Whistlefield I mentioned in the last chapter on the Gare Loch, the one from which there are such wonderful views of the three lochs, Gare, Goil and Long.

The steamer normally sails up Loch Goil to Lochgoilhead, then back to Loch Long and up to Arrochar, so we follow Loch Goil first. It is a fiord all the way up. Most of the mountains on either side are over 2,000 feet, but they look even higher since they rise so steeply from sea level.

About a mile up, on the west side, we see the ruined Carrick Castle. It stands on a rocky promontory, but at one time this was an island, and on the landward side there was a drawbridge. The castle was considered impregnable until the men of Athole took it from the Campbells in 1685 and burned it. Some say the original castle was built by the Vikings, and others that it was built by Robert the Bruce, when he was Earl of Carrick. But the most likely reason for the name is that the castle was built on a rock, and Carrick is a corruption of Craig, the Gaelic for a rock. Not far from the castle is Carrick Castle Hotel.

We sail up to Lochgoilhead and you'll be surprised to know that the mountains to the east are part of Glasgow. This is the Ardgoil Park of 15,000 acres, given to the city by the late Lord Rowallan in 1906. There were no hikers in Lord Rowallan's day—merely walkers. Youth hostellers were unknown, and mountaineering had not become the popular sport it is today. So Lord Rowallan was ahead of his time when he said, " As it is not possible for the public to have access to mountains in this neighbourhood, it seems to me desirable that our fellow citizens should have a mountain territory which will be their own for all time."

At Lochgoilhead you will see more of the mansions and villas which the merchants of Glasgow built as holiday houses in Victorian days. Lochgoilhead, however, is rather more remote than places like Cove, Kilcreggan, Strone and Blairmore. A road leads up the glen behind the village and parts at a cross-roads. One way takes you up to the Rest and Be Thankful in Glen Croe and so to Arrochar and back to Glasgow. The other is through Hell's Glen and takes you to the shore of Loch Fyne and so to Inveraray, where the Duke of Argyll lives.

We sail back down Loch Goil and round into Loch Long again. From here to Arrochar the loch is even narrower than Loch Goil. To our right we see the main road come down a hill and run along the lochside. Above it every now and then a plume of smoke shows that the train is peching up the West Highland Railway. The port and the oil tanks is Finnart, and you'll probably see an ocean-going oil tanker berthed there. This was once all wild country and the MacFarlane clan ruled the roost. They were as wild as the country, and so enjoyed marauding expeditions by night that the local saying was, " The MacFarlanes have the moon for their lantern."

Hell's Glen.

Scottish Tourist Board.

Arrochar.

Scottish Tourist Board.

To our left, where you see a very occasional building at the foot of the mountains, some 200 houses once stood. But the houses were emptied at the time of the Highland clearances, and the people went to Canada to make room for sheep.

The rafts and odd-looking apparatus that you see on the loch belong to the Admiralty's torpedo testing station at the top of Loch Long. But before we reach it we see Ardgartan on the west shore. You are certain to see caravans here, for this is the first and one of the biggest caravan camping sites in the whole of Britain. People from all over the world camp on this beautiful site.

Then we see the torpedo testing station on our left and the steamer swings into Arrochar pier. Arrochar is a pleasant little place, with hotels, boarding houses and tea rooms. It also has midges in the summer time, but it's not alone among Firth of Clyde places for that. There are also famous midges at Innellan, Tighnabruaich and Lagg in the Isle of Arran. Scottish scientists are studying the midge problem, and you'll be able to buy various sticks and ointments to keep the midges off. A cigar does the trick too.

Opposite Arrochar is one of the most famous of Scottish mountains, the Cobbler, 2,891 feet. From certain points in Arrochar you can see quite distinctly the figure of the Cobbler bending over his last, right on top of the mountain. Its real name is Ben Arthur, and some of the best climbing in Scotland is to be had on it. For ordinary people the best way up is to go round the head of the loch to Ardgartan and take to the hills on the right a little beyond the camping site. Don't try going straight up the Cobbler. It's difficult and dangerous. An old legend has it that each Duke of Argyll has to prove that he's fit for the job by climbing the mountain and putting his foot on the Cobbler's head. I have not heard of any Duke having done it in my time.

From Arrochar it's only a little more than a mile to Loch Lomond, and it's a favourite tour to sail up to Arrochar, cross over to Tarbet and then sail down Loch Lomond. In ancient days the Vikings did just this, but not as a holiday tour. They dragged their war galleys across the hill to Tarbet, relaunched them there, and then sailed up and down Loch Lomond sacking, burning and looting. When they were tired of raiding, they dragged their galleys and loot back to Arrochar and sailed away down Loch Long.

And we sail away down Loch Long too. But our journey is a peaceful one to the Coasts of Cowal.

CHAPTER SIX

THE COWAL COAST

Now we travel that delectable land between Strone Point and Toward Point, round the Holy Loch and along the Cowal coast. You can get to it by road, but the usual way is by steamer, and once again I'm going to assume that we see it from the deck. Dunoon is the capital of Cowal, and many people choose to take coaches from Dunoon to see the surrounding country, while the rich folk with a car take it across in the car ferry and arrange their own touring.

But we start from Strone. Steamers no longer use Strone pier, but there's a ferry across the mouth of the Holy Loch to Hunter's Quay. The Holy Loch itself is more like a deep bay than a loch. There are two stories about how the loch got its name. The one I like is that St. Mungo, the patron saint of Glasgow, sent to the Holy Land for some earth to place in the foundations of Glasgow Cathedral. On its way back with the precious soil, the ship sheltered from a storm in this loch. But the storm was so fierce that the ship sank and most of the soil was lost. So, since the holy soil was at the bottom of the bay, it was called the Holy Loch. What little soil was salvaged was brought ashore where Kilmun stands now and used as a foundation for the old kirk there.

But Kilmun in the Gaelic means " the church of Mun," and the other (and I regret to say more likely) theory is that the Holy Loch was so called because St. Fintan Munnu— " Mun " for short—lived there. He was a follower of St. Columba in the sixth century and built his cell at Kilmun.

You'll maybe see some laid-up ships in the Holy Loch and if you're fairly early in the summer, a South Georgian whaler or two. The whalers are often laid up here during the summer, before they go to refit for their adventurous voyage. During the war the Holy Loch was a submarine base.

Kilmun is a holiday place with a pier for Clyde steamers and a ferry across the Holy Loch to Ardnadam. Robert Napier, the great engineer, bought an estate here and built the first houses in the village. They are just north of the pier and are known as the "Six Canisters." Napier had a better eye for engineering than for architecture.

Beside Kilmun Church there is an old tower, which is all that remains of the Collegiate Church founded in 1442 by Sir Duncan Campbell of Lochow. He was called Duncan the Prosperous and was the first Lord Campbell. The Dukes of Argyll are his descendants, and the mausoleum in the grounds is the burial place of the Argyll family.

At the top of the loch is the Cothouse Inn, by the River Echaig flowing from Loch Eck. This part of the Firth of Clyde is very mild, and really stern Scots have been known to complain that it's too warm! The road forks here. Straight on is Loch Eck, by way of Benmore estate (now a big Forestry School), and Inverchapel, home of the late Baron Inverchapel who, as Sir James Clark Kerr, was Britain's ambassador in Moscow, Chungking, Java and New York.

Between Benmore and Inverchapel lies Puck's Glen, just on the right of the road. This is a small and lovely natural park, with paths built round a gorge and a rest hut panelled with wood representing every variety of tree found on the Benmore estate. It is in memory of a former " King's Botanist for Scotland," Sir I. Bayley Balfour.

Loch Eck is worth seeing. It is long and narrow and beautiful. There is a hotel at Coylett and there ought to be a memorial to the Coylett man who boasted that he had smoked tobacco for over 100 years. His name was James Grieve and he is buried at Kilmun. His gravestone records that he died at the age of 111, so it's quite possible that he smoked for a century. About half way up Loch Eck is Whistlefield and the road on the right is the one Sir Harry Lauder would take if he went " ower the hill tae Ardentinny, just to see his bonny Jeannie."

A steamer sailed regularly on Loch Eck within the memory of man, and it was the place where David Napier sailed the first iron steamer in the world. The date was 1820 and the ship was named the " Aglaia." If we go right on up Loch Eck we reach Strachur on the shore of Loch Fyne and pass the memorial at Glenbranter that Sir Harry Lauder put up to his only son, killed in the First World War.

But this is a far cry from Kilmun, and we must get back to the top of the Holy Loch and continue our journey round it. As you turn south for Dunoon there is a road on the right which leads to wonderful scenery and lonely, lovely Glendaruel. You must have heard (or, if you haven't, you must hear) Mrs. Kennedy Fraser's version of the old song, " Glendaruel," which tells the story of Deirdre, the beautiful Irish princess who fled there with her lover.

Glendaruel, like Kilmun, has two versions of the origin of its name. The poetic one is " the fold of sleep." The dramatic one is that, when the Vikings and the Gaels fought up and down the River Ruel in the old times, so many bodies went into the burn that it ran red with blood. So Glendaruel means " the glen of red blood."

Down the Holy Loch the first village is Sandbank, famous for yacht building—though maybe the Robertson yard won't want to be reminded that the " Sceptre," beaten by " Columbia " in the America's Cup races off Rhode Island, U.S.A., was built here.

From Sandbank there are two ways to Dunoon—the high road inland, which goes by charming Loch Loskin, and the shore road by Ardnadam, Hunter's Quay and Kirn. We keep to the shore and, just as we leave the Holy Loch, we come to Hunter's Quay.

Hunter's Quay is named after the local laird, Robert Hunter of Hafton, who built the first real pier at Dunoon.

H

THE ROYAL MARINE HOTEL
HUNTER'S QUAY

A.A.
—— *THE HOTEL ON THE CLYDE*
R.A.C.

Tel. Dunoon 1001/2   *Prop.* T. E. WEIR

At the pier is the Royal Marine Hotel and the headquarters of the Royal Clyde Yacht Club, the same building but with separate entrances. This is a great place during the famous Clyde Fortnight, one of the biggest yachting events in Britain. The Fortnight is in July and yachtsmen from all over the world come here to race. The big event is the series of races for the Seawanhaka Cup for six-metre yachts steered and crewed by amateurs.

From Hunter's Quay to Dunoon is an almost unbroken line of villas, hotels, mansions, boarding houses, cottages, and even a tenement. But don't make the mistake of thinking this is all the same place. The people who go to Hunter's Quay consider they are in quite a different place from Kirn. Kirn is the next pier towards Dunoon, and if you are in doubt, you can always tell the places by the name on the pier!

Behind Kirn is the place where the great bare-knuckle fight for the championship of Britain was held, between John Goudie of Scotland and Ned Langlands of England. Nobody is absolutely sure of the date, about the middle of last century, and nobody knows who won. But it's said that the Fancy came from all over the British Isles to see the match, and that it was a great fight. The site of the fight is now the Cowal Golf Course, and before that it was the Farm of Ardenslate, where Roman remains were dug up between the championship fight and the time the farm was turned into a golf course.

Now we come by the East Bay into Dunoon pier. You can see right away that this is really a holiday resort. Its population in the winter is around 9,000. In summer it goes up to over 30,000. Music greets the steamer as she sidles alongside the pier. As I've said, we don't have English-style piers on the Firth of Clyde, but Dunoon pier has a balcony promenade, from which you can watch the steamers arriving and departing, and also one or two shops and a tea room.

Some 120 years ago you wouldn't have landed on a pier here. You'd have got into a small boat and been ferried to a jetty. This wooden jetty, some 130 yards in length, was built in 1835 by men who realised that the little village had a big future. The jetty was replaced by a proper pier, built by the famous Stevenson family to the order of Robert Hunter. The Stevensons built piers, lighthouses and break- waters. They also, as it were, built Robert Louis Stevenson, and he lived at Dunoon during the building of the pier. The present pier is a reconstruction of the Stevenson one. Dunoon Town Council spent £50,000 on it in 1898—which was a lot of money then!

Facing the pier are the Castle Gardens and you may imagine that the castellated building you see on the height behind the Gardens is Dunoon Castle. But it is actually the Dunoon Town Council Chambers. It was originally the mansion house of a Lord Provost of Glasgow, James Ewing, and his building it in 1822 helped to turn the fortunes of Dunoon from " A small decayed village " (a description of it in that very year) to the modern holiday resort.

To the right is Dunoon Pavilion, a new theatre and ball- room which replaces one burnt down after the Second World War. To the right is also the town's information kiosk, the parking place for motor coaches which will take you through the Highlands, the shopping centre, and the East Bay connecting with Kirn.

Dunoon

The road behind the town takes you to the Cowal Games park. This is one of the greatest Highland Gatherings held in Scotland. It takes place on two days towards the end of August and the town is decorated with banners of every clan tartan there is. For 40 years the World's Championship Pipe Band Contest was fought out here. Now the contest takes place in various parts of Scotland, but Dunoon is still famous for the huge number of pipe bands who turn out for the Cowal Games. The climax of the Games is the march of a thousand pipers, all blowing at once.

If we return to Dunoon pier and look south, we see the rock upon which Dunoon Castle was built and, half way up that rock, the statue of Highland Mary, looking towards the coast of Ayrshire, where she met Robert Burns. This is one of the great mysteries of the Burns story. Even the most expert of the experts cannot agree on exactly what happened between Robert Burns and Highland Mary. There is general agreement that she was the great early love of his life, and many years after she died and he was married to Jean Armour, he wrote the famous poem, " To Mary in Heaven."

Highland Mary was Mary Campbell and she was born in a thatched cottage at Auchamore Farm, just over a mile behind Dunoon. When she was a young girl, she went to work in Ayrshire, either as a dairymaid at Coilsfield or a nursemaid in Mauchline. She was either innocent or rather giddy (I can't help these alternatives; the experts just won't agree!), but it seems certain that she fell in love with Robert Burns. She and Robert exchanged Bibles over running water and so considered themselves married in the " Scotch style." Later she left Ayrshire to see her parents in Dunoon. She got only as far as Greenock, when she died of a fever. As I've already mentioned in my Greenock section, her grave is there today. Her birthplace in Dunoon, on the other hand, has long been swept away.

Only a few stones of Dunoon Castle remain. It's said that the first castle here was erected in the sixth century. About 1300 it was known as " the Capital Castle of the Lordship of Cowal." It was held by an English garrison when Robert the Steward, son of the daughter of Robert the Bruce, took it by sword and drove the Sassenachs out. In this affray he was ably assisted by Sir Colin Campbell (founder of the Argyll family), so when, years later, he became King Robert the Second, he made Sir Colin hereditary keeper of Dunoon Castle. Up to that time the lands had belonged to the Lamonts, and now a feud started between the Lamonts and the Campbells. Repeatedly the Campbells won, and the Lamonts were forced to retire to their castle at Toward.

Mary Queen of Scots visited Dunoon in 1563 and stayed at the castle for two days. Her sister, Lady Jane Stewart, was the wife of Archibald, Earl of Argyll, and was in residence there.

In 1646 the feud between the Campbells and the Lamonts came to a head. The Campbells besieged the Lamonts in Toward Castle, but the Lamonts held fast. Then the Campbells suggested an armistice. The Lamonts agreed but, as soon as their defences were down, the Campbells imprisoned the garrison and their families, plundered the land round about, and then carried all their prisoners to Dunoon Castle. There the 36 most important Lamonts were hanged and some hundreds of others were shot and thrown into a pit. Their bones were discovered at the beginning of this century when a new road was being made.

Perhaps the thought of their own perfidy and the knowledge that slain Lamonts lay near the castle was too much for the Argyll family, but they decided to move the seat of the Earl of Argyll from Dunoon to Inveraray on Loch Fyne, where it is today and can be visited by coach tour from Dunoon. After the Argylls left, Dunoon Castle was allowed to fall into ruin, and Dunoon itself became a forgotten clachan until the Glasgow merchants revived it.

From Castle Hill the promenade runs round the West Bay to the Bullwood. Behind the promenade is an almost unbroken line of hotels and boarding houses which were once the seaside villas of these same Glasgow merchants. No traffic is allowed along the promenade and probably the best boating on the Clyde is to be had here. The beach is pebbly, but there is sand at the Lido, a bathing station. Behind the Lido is a favourite walking place, Morag's Fairy Glen. This is really a wild park and there are paths up the glen by waterfalls. A favourite ballad in these parts is entitled " Morag's Fairy Glen." It's written by William Cameron and I give two of the verses here:—

> There's music in the wild cascade,
>   There's love amang the trees,
> There's beauty in ilk bank an' brae,
>   An' balm upon the breeze;

Then, meet me, love, by a' unseen
    Beside yon mossy den;
O! Meet me, love, at dewy eve,
    In Morag's Fairy Glen.

You may well hear that sung in Dunoon Pavilion.
Now we go back to Dunoon pier and sail for Innellan.
The rocks with the lighthouse on them are the Gantocks.
They look nothing from the steamer deck, but they have
wrecked many a ship. Only a few years ago a Swedish
cargo ship, full of iron ore, ran on to the Gantocks and
then sank with a loss of several lives. For some time her
masts could be seen above the water at low tide. Efforts
were made to salvage her, but her iron cargo kept her down.

Looking shorewards you see the line of hotels and
boarding houses round the West Bay. Past the Bathing Lido
you see a large white house, almost the last one in the
burgh of Dunoon. This is Laudervale, now a hotel but
once the residence of Sir Harry Lauder.

We approach Innellan pier. The village was started by
the merchants of Greenock as a holiday place. The big
white hotel on the hillside has one of the best views of the
Firth of Clyde, and also television for those who are
sated with outdoor views! The houses here are built on
terraces, and this is one of the best places to see the ships
of the world sail up and down the Firth.

Innellan is the place where the blind parish minister, the
Rev. George Matheson, wrote that famous hymn, " O, Love
that will not let me go." He became blind at the age of 18
and wrote it in " extreme mental distress." The organist
of Glasgow Cathedral wrote the tune for it when he was
on holiday in Brodick in 1884. Matheson himself left
Innellan Parish Church to become minister of a kirk in
Edinburgh, and ended his days high in the Church of
Scotland.

Past Innellan, with the one natural sandy beach on the
Cowal shore, the houses become fewer and then we see the
lighthouse at Toward Point, with the little village of
Toward around it. The ruins of Toward Castle where the

Campbells besieged the Lamonts, are about a mile on the road past Toward Point.

Any steamer going round Toward Point is almost certain to be making for Rothesay, and soon you see Rothesay Bay to the south. On the Cowal shore to the north there is a big mansion, known as Castle Toward. It was built for one of Glasgow's most enterprising Provosts, Kirkman Finlay, by one of Glasgow's best architects, David Hamilton. Some people confuse Castle Toward with Toward Castle, not surprisingly, but the mansion was built in 1832. It was owned privately until Glasgow Corporation took it over as a holiday school for Glasgow children. One very popular school held there every summer is an orchestral course. This course ends with a symphony concert by the pupils in Dunoon Pavilion, and the standard is remarkably high. Well-known conductors come down to Castle Toward to take the final rehearsals and conduct the concert at Dunoon.

If you are travelling by road round the Cowal coast, you go on to the shore of Loch Striven. But Loch Striven belongs to another chapter, and we'll end our look at the Cowal Coast here.

' *Queen Mary II.* '   *British Railways.*

CHAPTER SEVEN

DEFEAT OF THE VIKINGS

W E cross again from the Highland side of the Firth of Clyde to the Lowland. While the Gaelic-speaking clansmen of the Cowal coast were killing each other, life was comparatively quiet among the Lowland farmers and crafts-men on the Ayrshire coast. But it was not ever thus. The Vikings came to the Clyde and ravaged the Lowlands as much as the Highlands. They had pretended to the owner-ship of the islands of Scotland for some 400 years, and it all ended at Largs.

In my chapter on " The Ports of the Clyde " I took you down past Wemyss Bay to the point where we could see Largs. The steamer sails into Largs Bay to a pier which almost qualifies as one of the ports. It is, in fact, the port for the Great Cumbrae Island, lying just across a strait a little more than a mile long. There is a ferry service from Largs to Millport, the capital of the Cumbraes.

Even as the ropes are thrown from the steamer to the pier, you can see that Largs is a holiday resort. It is one of the " Big Three " of the Clyde; the others are Dunoon and Rothesay. Largs has the advantage that it can be reached by road and rail from the Glasgow area, and so it is tre-mendously popular with day trippers. In certain aspects, particularly on a bright, sunny day, it has an almost conti-nental look. This is partly because the Italians have built two enormous cafés on the sea front, and other people have tended to follow their example and go in for bright colours, lots of glass, and even striped umbrellas and awnings. Largs is one of the few places on the Clyde where there are open-air cafés.

Largs.

L. S. Paterson.

The original village of Largs stood between two burns, the Noddle and the Gogo. Now it extends considerably north and south, and goes back as far as the steep hill behind it will allow. The long white building you see as you sail towards Largs was built as the Hollywood Hotel. During the Second World War it became a naval headquarters. Now it is a home for old folk. Behind it is Routenburn golf course and, seen on the road but hidden from the steamer, is Netherhall, once the summer home of one of the world's great scientists, Lord Kelvin. If you go up the Noddle Valley you'll also see Brisbane House, which was the birthplace of Sir Thomas Brisbane, who was Governor of New South Wales from 1821 to 1825, and after whom the Australian city was named.

Right in the middle of Largs, reached by a little lane, is the Skelmorlie Aisle, which is a relic of a much older church than the parish kirk alongside the Aisle. Sir Robert Montgomery of Skelmorlie built this Aisle as a mausoleum in 1636 and you'll see the monument to Sir Robert and Margaret, his wife, there. A painted roof shows a horse kicking a lady, the 12 signs of the Zodiac, and various views of Skelmorlie Castle. Sir Hew Montgomery, one of the heroes of Chevy Chase in 1388, is said to be buried in the Skelmorlie Aisle.

Largs was the home of the Royal Clyde Yacht Club, the second oldest on the Clyde, but, as I've mentioned, that Club's headquarters are now at Hunter's Quay. However, there is a Royal Largs Yacht Club, and there is also a great interest in the sport of sailing catamarans, one new to the Clyde and being taken up enthusiastically as far away as Arran.

Across the Gogo Burn a line of fine hotels stretches on top of the Broomfields, and then the Bowencraig Walk takes you to the "Pencil," which is the popular name given to the Battle of Largs Memorial on the shore. Sailing from Largs we make for the Cumbrae side so, if you want a close look at the Pencil, you must take this shore walk.

The Memorial was erected in 1912 to commemorate a battle which was fought in 1263. In the autumn of that year King Haakon brought a great fleet of Viking galleys to the Firth of Clyde. He was determined to prove once and for all his claim to the Scottish Islands. King Alexander III learned that he was in the Clyde—indeed, his fleet were as far south as Lamlash in Arran and as far north as Loch Long. But the main warships were in the sheltered waters between the Cumbrae Islands and Largs. So Alexander mustered as big a Scottish army as he could—though it can't have been a very big one, as his cavalry numbered a mere 1,500—and took up positions where the Douglas Park lies now, just behind Largs.

First of all, the Scots tried to argue Haakon out of his pretensions. He refused to budge. Both sides prepared for battle and then, on the night of October 1, a storm blew up and drove a number of the Viking ships ashore. Haakon decided to turn this reverse to profit, and ordered a landing. But as the Vikings were mustering on this ground near

Bowen Craig, the Scots came thundering down upon them.
At dawn they saw their enemies upon the shore and so they
attacked. The fighting lasted all that day, but so did the
storm, and Haakon's fleet at sea were unable to help the
men ashore.

By the time night fell the Scots had won the Battle of
Largs. The remnants of the Viking army took to their
boats. Next day King Haakon asked King Alexander's
permission to bury his dead. Some were buried at Largs,
and some on the Great and Little Cumbraes. The Viking
fleet then left the Clyde and sailed back to Norway. There,
not long afterwards, King Haakon died, some say of a
broken heart. And thereafter the whole of Scotland
belonged to the Scots.

Now, though the steamer is sailing to the Great Cumbrae,
we'll keep to the shore. We're approaching Fairlie, the
village which refused to be described as a town. British
Railways, deciding that they should make quite clear which
Fairlie station was which, put up a notice in the landward
one saying " Fairlie Town," and one at the other saying
" Fairlie Pier." But the good folk of Fairlie said this was
daft. Fairlie wasn't a town. So the notice was taken down,
a new one put up saying " Fairlie High," and presumably
everybody was satisfied.

Before we get to Fairlie we see Kelburne Castle, the home
of the Earl of Glasgow. The original castle was built in the
16th century, but has been considerably altered since then.
There is, by the way, a tea room at the top of the Haylie
Brae behind Largs. This tea room was started by the Earl
of Glasgow's daughters. They don't own it now, but it is
still there, with enchanting views of the Clyde.

Fairlie is, at the moment of writing, a seaside resort, the
winter port for steamers to the Isle of Arran, a dormitory
for West of Scotland business men, a good place for rose
growing, and a world-famous place for yacht building.
I have to say " at the moment of writing," because nobody
knows exactly what its future is going to be. It has been
announced that Fairlie has been chosen as the site for a

N.A.T.O. naval base. (The N.A.T.O. Fleet mustered here a few summers ago and the Powers That Be must have been impressed.)

At first it was thought that this would mean a huge establishment, but now it's understood that a boom will be built, a small headquarters set up in Fairlie, and nothing else unless a war comes along. Fervently we hope that the Fairlie N.A.T.O. base is never used. But, if you see some building in progress, you'll know what it is.

In the summer time you may see as many as 100 or more yachts at moorings off Fairlie. The large building beside the pier is Fife's yacht-building yard and Captain James Williamson, in *The Clyde Passenger Steamer*, says that Fairlie might have become an important shipbuilding yard if the first Fife had not been so determined to build yachts. In 1814 this yard built the " Industry," the seventh steamer to be made on the Clyde. It was such a success that the syndicate of business men for whom it was built wanted Fife to make more steamers and offered to set up a big shipbuilding yard for him.

But Fife said " No." All he wanted to do was build yachts. So it's been yachts ever since, and the name of Fife is honoured by yachtsmen along with McGruer of Clynder, Robertson of Sandbank, and Silver of Rosneath.

There's an odd story of William Fife that has a special interest in view of the " Sceptre's " display against the " Columbia " in the America's Cup. I've mentioned that Lord Kelvin lived at Largs during the summer. He knew Fife well and had many an argument with him about the design of yachts. One day he drew on the Fairlie sand the outlines of his ideal yacht. Fife immediately countered with a design in pebbles of *his* perfect yacht. The tide washed the designs away, but the two yachts were built, one according to the theories of Lord Kelvin, the other according to the practice of William Fife. Once they were in the water the Kelvin yacht could never beat the Fife yacht.

Near Fairlie High station is Fairlie Glen, and there are the ruins of Fairlie Castle, built in 1521. Literary tourists

may know Lady Wardlaw's " Ballad of Hardyknute,"
which tells the story of the Battle of Largs. She was an
18th century poetess, and she brought Fairlie Castle into
the battle. But, as the battle took place in 1263 and the
castle wasn't built until 1521, this must be attributed to
poetic licence.

Soon after it leaves Fairlie, the road goes inland from
the Firth and climbs the hill to West Kilbride. Between the
road and the water lies Hunterston Estate, once just an
estate but now partly occupied by the huge Nuclear Power
Station. You will have seen the great buildings to the
south as you left Fairlie. Even from across the water on the
Cumbrae side, they dominate the coastline. It is said that
at Millport an enterprising man has set up a telescope, so
that holiday-makers can see, for a small charge, how the
Nuclear Power Station is getting on.

By the time you read this it may be complete. At the
moment we don't know how it is going to fit in with the
scenery. But at least it is known that the nuclear power to
be made there is for peaceful purposes.

Before these building operations there was a path which
led round the shore to the clachan and castle of Portencross.
This 12th century castle was supposed to be the twin of the
one you can see on the Little Cumbrae, and was one of the
" guardians " of the Clyde.

And now we go back to Largs and sail from the pier to
the Great Cumbrae, either by steamer or by one of the little
ferry vessels. The Great and Little Cumbraes were two of
the islands which King Haakon laid claim to. One story is
that most of his army camped on the Great Cumbrae and
they held some kind of religious ceremony before the
Battle of Largs. But Thor and Odin did not prevail that
day.

The Great Cumbrae is three and a half miles long, and
about 11 miles round. It is famous for children and bicycles,
but lately motorists have been taking their cars over. The
golf course is on a hill and apparently golfers must have
some form of transport to get to it!

We sail quite near the Cumbrae shore and someone on deck is sure to point out the Lion Rock to you, if you haven't noticed it first. From the deck this odd piece of rock looks very like a lion indeed, and for fully a minute or so. It's easy to see the likeness on the island itself. Not far away is another wall of rock, and in the old days the natives of Cumbrae called this the Fairy Dyke, and knew the Lion Rock as the De'il's Dyke. The story was that the Cumbrae fairies decided to build a bridge to the mainland, so that they could go over to visit their friends. While they were at work, the De'il himself came by and asked what they were doing. When they told him, he said he could build a far better bridge than they could, and he started right away.

The De'il had built quite a piece of bridge when he heard the fairies laughing. He found they were laughing at his handiwork, which was all squint, while theirs was true and straight. This so enraged him that he raised his right hoof and hit his bridge one tremendous kick. It tumbled into the form we see today. Which is all right, as far as it goes, but no native goes on to tell why the fairies didn't finish *their* bridge.

We sail into Keppel Pier and, if you are landing on the Great Cumbrae, you should make certain whether the steamer is going on to Millport pier or not. Keppel is not far from Millport and there are taxis and buses to take you there.

The red buildings behind the pier are the Scottish Marine Biological Station and Museum. The museum is well worth visiting. Every kind of fish and aquatic specimen in the whole of the Firth of Clyde is represented here and you'll be astonished at the variety. You'll even see an octopus, a rather charming one. Valuable research work is done at the Biological Station, which is considered one of the best in Britain.

We sail round Farland Point and into Millport Bay, which is really three bays with fine sandy beaches. The houses line the shore and the hills rise pleasantly behind them. There are some small rocky islands protecting the

Millport.   *Scottish Tourist Board.*

pier and the central bay and motor boats take parties round them.

Millport has an Early Victorian appearance and it was even more so when the horse carriages and waggonettes were drawn up at the pierhead to take the passengers to their hotels or for a trip round the island. Now we'll be very lucky indeed if we see the last remaining carriage.

Everything seems so pleasant and quiet here that it's difficult to believe that the famous Battle of Millport took place just over 50 years ago. It was more in the style of the Battle of Garelochhead than the Battle of Largs, however. Millport Town Council had a dispute with the railway companies about paying for the reconstruction of the pier. It reached such a pitch that the companies threatened to remove the steamer service, so that Millportians and holiday-makers would be marooned on the island. It was in the middle of July and the Great Cumbrae was as packed with people as it could be.

Millport town council were not moved by these threats and the morning came when the companies ordered their steamers to cease calling at Millport. Their reply was to organise a scratch fleet of fishing and motor boats, and they got everyone across to the mainland who wanted to go. In a day or two the railway companies succumbed to public outcry, and the steamer services were resumed.

Millport is another of the Clyde resorts which exercises a remarkable fascination on west of Scotland people. Families go there year after year and there is a secret society known as the Millport Rats, composed mainly of Glasgow men.

A long promenade runs round the three bays, and in the centre is the Priory, once a private mansion and now a public park. Behind are the plain Parish Kirk and the gothic Cathedral of Argyll and the Isles. The Cathedral looks like a 13th century building, but it was actually designed by Butterfield in 1849. It was first of all an Episcopal collegiate church, but in 1876 it was consecrated as a cathedral.

In the Parish Church kirkyard you may still be able to see the tombstone of the famous minister, the Rev. James Adam, who prayed every Sunday for " the Great and Little Cumbrae, and the adjacent islands of Great Britain and Ireland." He was a remarkable character and wrote the inscription on the stone. It runs in part:—

Erected in Memory of the

Rev. James Adam,

Late Minister in Cumbray,

Born in the Year 1748; Licensed in 1773; Ordained in 1799;

Died in June, 1831.

Here on a cold, damp bed he lies,

Without a friend to close his eyes,

Wrapt in his usual unsocial pride,

Indifferent to all the world beside.

The usual way to go round the Great Cumbrae from Millport is counter-clockwise. You go right along the promenade, past the Crocodile Rock—a great favourite with children, because it is painted in bright colours to look like the crocodile in " Peter Pan." Then out to Keppel and by the Fairy Dyke and the Lion Rock. About half a mile north of the Lion Rock is Ballykellet, where an ancient mansion belonging to the Montgomery family once stood. Here lived Dame Margaret Montgomery who was thrown from her horse when she was visiting Largs. When she tried to catch it, the horse kicked her and she died. She is the woman represented in the painting on the ceiling of the Skelmorlie Aisle in Largs.

κ

The road goes to the most northerly point of the island, Tomont End. An obelisk stands there in memory of two young midshipmen of H.M.S. " Shearwater," who were drowned when their boat capsized off Tomont End in May, 1884.

Down the west side of the island there are beautiful views of the Isle of Bute. The village straight across the water is Kilchattan Bay, where the Navy are rebuilding the pier. As you go south the great mountains of the Isle of Arran face you, and as you walk (or drive) round to Millport, you see the Little Cumbrae across the channel which the steamers take to Arran.

You can visit the Little Cumbrae from Millport by hiring a boat. The only inhabited buildings on the island are a farmhouse on the east side and the Cumbrae Light-

Firth of Clyde near Wemyss Bay.

Scottish Tourist Board.

house, one of the most important in the chain of light-houses around the Firth of Clyde. On an islet by the farmhouse are the ruins of the castle which is the twin of the one over the water at Portencross. Little is known of this castle except that it was used by Robert the Second in the 14th century and that Cromwell destroyed it in 1653. Near the castle are the remains of an ancient chapel dedicated to St. Vey, a disciple of St. Columba who had come from Iona.

On the very top of the island, 409 feet up, is a tower which was once the second lighthouse to be built in Scotland. It was made in 1755 and it was lit by a coal fire in a huge grate. The Lighthouse Commissioners found, however, that it was badly placed and so they built the present Cumbrae Lighthouse in 1793.

Once again we look across at the Isle of Bute, and it's there we go in my next chapter.

CHAPTER EIGHT

THE ISLE OF SAINTS

THE steamer sails round Toward Point on the Cowal coast and into sweet Rothesay Bay. It maybe doesn't look exactly sweet. Indeed, it's probably bustling with boats and steamers, because Rothesay is immensely popular in the holiday season. But it gets the adjective because of a much-sung Victorian ballad entitled "Sweet Rothesay Bay." One verse will give you the idea:—

> It's a bonnie bay i' the mornin',
>   An' bonnier at the noon;
> But bonniest when the sun draps
>   An' red comes up the moon:
> When the mist creeps ower the Cumbraes
>   An' Arran peaks are grey;
> An' the great black hills, like sleepin' kings,
>   Sit grand roun' Rothesay Bay.

This, as in most Victorian ballads, is a rather fanciful description. Rothesay is the capital of the Isle of Bute, and the highest hill on the island is not much more than 900 feet. Bute is the second largest island in the Firth of Clyde, and though it is much smaller, its population is about three times that of the Isle of Arran. Indeed, Arran (and also the Cumbraes) is administered from Rothesay.

Arran is towering and majestic. Bute is low lying and pleasant. Its temperature is so equable that Rothesay is known as the Madeira of Scotland. This is not because it takes the cake, as many a Scotch comic has said. It is a

Rothesay Publicity.

Rothesay Bay.

charming, " easy " island and it certainly appealed to the saints who came across the water to convert the Scots to Christianity. Among the holy people commemorated on Bute by place names and chapel ruins are St. Blane, St. Brendan, St. Ninian, St. Cormac, St. Mary, St. Colmac, St. Marnock and St. Michael. It's obvious that, when the saints came marching in, they knew a good place when they saw one.

The Isle of Bute is about 15½ miles long, but the Round Bute bus tour covers only 23 miles. This is because there is no road round the northern third of the island, and a considerable part of the south is also roadless.

The capital, Rothesay, is one of the best-set towns on the Firth of Clyde. The houses line Rothesay Bay and climb high up the hills that shelter the town on the west and south. The steamer comes into Rothesay pier, which is every bit as busy as Dunoon's. It's said that Rothesay was the first place on the Firth to have a quay of any sort. This was in the 11th century, so you mustn't expect to see any of it now.

Rothesay is given over almost entirely to holiday-makers and there are long promenades stretching north and south. There are Winter Gardens, a Pavilion, cinemas, putting greens, tennis courts, fun fairs, an open-air Bathing Lido and an indoor swimming pool, and a golf course with some of the most glorious views of the Firth. Palm trees grow along the promenade as you can see. You'll find palm trees in several places on the Clyde. This is the outward evidence of the influence of the Gulf Stream in these parts.

Up a narrow street from the pier are the ruins of Rothesay Castle, now enclosed by modern buildings—I mean by comparison with the castle, which is said to have been founded by King Magnus Barefoot, the Viking, in the 11th century. The castle is surrounded by a moat and you go in to visit it by a drawbridge.

Like so many other castles in this part of the world, it was repeatedly besieged, captured, retaken, burnt down and so on. Magnus Barefoot was thrown out by the Scots, but in the 13th century Haakon of Norway retook it. He

Rothesay Castle.

Rothesay Publicity Committee.

held it only until his defeat at the Battle of Largs, when the Scots occupied it once more. Then the English turned the Scots out in the 14th century, and Robert the Bruce's men had to win it back. King Robert the Second added considerably to the castle and enjoyed staying there. He made his son Duke of Rothesay, and to perfervid Scots (and by the law of the land) the present Prince of Wales is the Duke of Rothesay. King Robert the Third, who made Rothesay a Royal Burgh in 1400, died in the castle—of a broken heart, they say.

Rothesay Castle is yet another of the ruins that Cromwell knocked abaht a bit. His troops set it alight in 1650. The ruin was completed in 1685 by a brother of the Earl of Argyll. Since 1874 various Marquesses of Bute have helped to restore the grounds and the castle, and you will find, as did Her Majesty the Queen and the Duke of Edinburgh, it worth visiting. In particular, you will see the ruined stairway behind the chapel known as the " Bluidy Stair." This is supposed to be the spot where the daughter of the High Steward of Scotland stabbed herself to death rather than submit to the Viking conqueror who had murdered her father and brothers in capturing the castle.

The ghost of Lady Isobel is seen, according to a 19th century ballad, which says—

> Aft in the mirk and midnicht hour
>   When a' is silent there,
> A shriek is heard and a ladye is seen
>   On the steps o' the Bluidy Stair.

I cannot, however, trace any record of this ghost having been seen, except by the ballad writer.

Not far from the castle is the old mill, where a cotton industry was established in 1778. David Dale, the Glasgow merchant, industrialist and benefactor, kept it going but it faded away as the West of Scotland lost the cotton business to India. In recent years it was revived as a tweed mill by the father of the present Marquis of Bute, and Bute tweeds are now so highly regarded that they have been used by such leading French fashion designers as Dior and Balmain.

You can go by the mill to the country road which leads to Loch Fad, the principal loch on the island. Many people take this road to see Kean's Cottage, otherwise Woodend House. The actor, Edmund Kean, was a moody man and he built this cottage in 1827 on the shore of Loch Fad to escape from the world. Like many another actor, he found he didn't really want to escape from the world after all, and he didn't live much in his cottage. The gateposts are surmounted by four busts. It's difficult now to make out their identities, but one is Shakespeare and another is Kean.

The Round Bute tour by bus can be highly recommended, for all the drivers act as guides as well, and some of them are very witty guides. We'll adopt our customary island procedure and go round Bute counter-clockwise. We go north from Rothesay pier. There is an almost unbroken line of houses and hotels from Rothesay to Port Bannatyne. One break is at the Skeoch Woods, a famous part that you are bound to hear mentioned several times a night by the Rothesay Entertainers in the Winter Gardens.

We go round Ardbeg Point and into Port Bannatyne, smaller and less pretentious than Rothesay, on Kames Bay. Here, as on the Holy Loch, you may see the South Georgian whalers laid up for the summer.

The customary route is inland, by Kames Castle to Ettrick Bay, but we continue on the road to Rhudabodach, along the first leg of the Kyles of Bute. From Rhudabodach a ferry crosses to Colintraive on the mainland at the very place where the Butemen used to swim their cattle across the " Narrows." Since you can see all this scene from the Kyles of Bute steamer, I won't describe it until the next chapter. The road goes only a little farther than Rhudabodach, so we'll retrace our steps to Port Bannatyne.

As you start on the road to Ettrick Bay, you see Kames Castle on your right. The main tower is a 14th century building and the low houses built around it were added much later. It belongs to the Bute family, as does Wester Kames, a peel tower not far from the castle and said to be the oldest inhabited house in Scotland. The lairds in this district were the Bannatynes, after whom Port Bannatyne is named. But Wester Kames was the home of a family named Spens. As in the case of Rothesay Castle, both these buildings have been preserved by the Marquesses of Bute.

Once upon a time an electric tram ran all the way from Rothesay to Ettrick Bay, and there was talk of developing this fine stretch of shore as a new seaside resort. But nothing came of the plans and the beach is still unspoiled. There is a tea room here and a children's playground, and the rest is left to Nature. Near Ettrick Bay are the remains of a hill fort and some Druidical circles. The Isle of Bute is full of such relics of times gone by.

The road north from Ettrick Bay is similar to the one north from Port Bannatyne. It leads to St. Michael's Chapel and no farther. For the south we must go back towards Port Bannatyne and then turn towards St. Ninian's Bay. From here, if conditions are right, you may get a boat across to the calf of Bute, Inch Marnock. This island is farmed now, but once it was known as the Drunkard's Isle because Bute people had a rough and ready way of dealing with their alcoholics. They rowed them across to Inch Marnock and marooned them there. When they thought the drunkards had been " cured," they returned to pick them up once again.

From St. Ninian's Bay we go inland and then south to Scalpsie Bay. This is another of the fine bathing beaches of Bute, and you can reach it direct from Rothesay by way of Loch Fad.

South again we go, till we come to the crossroads at Kingarth Church. The main road goes on to Kilchattan Bay, but we take the secondary road to the right and go down towards Garroch Head, the most southerly point of Bute. This brings us to the Chapel of St. Blane, and you can see that the saint had a great eye for a view. The aspect of Arran from this spot is about the best to be had in the whole of Bute. Beside St. Blane's Chapel two cemeteries will be pointed out to you, one on a higher level than the other. The higher is meant for men, the lower for women.

For the reason, we have to go back to the time when the chapel was being built, about nine centuries ago. As was the way in those bygone days, St. Blane wanted the foundations of his church to be in holy ground. He had some consecrated earth brought from Rome and taken ashore from the ship at Kilchattan Bay. The earth was placed in creels and these were slung over the backs of horses. They had not gone far before the back-band on one of the horses broke. St. Blane looked for help and saw a woman gathering shellfish not far away. He asked her for her belt to replace the broken back-band, but she refused to hand it over. So the saint vowed that no woman would ever lie in the holy earth. The cemetery was made on two levels, and the consecrated earth was put only on the higher ground. No woman was to be buried there. This is a very good story and maybe I shouldn't tell you that women have crept into the higher ground after all! In fact, they have been there since 1661.

You will also be shown (if you're on the Round Bute tour, anyway) a circular enclosure near the chapel called the Cauldron. This is supposed to have been a place of penance in the Middle Ages, though some people called it the Devil's Cauldron and said that this was where Auld Nick boiled his tougher victims before carrying them down below. It's thought, however, that the Cauldron was where people were put who had deeply offended the church. They were condemned to remain there for so many days, without either food or sleep. A number would be put in at one time and they had to keep each other awake during the whole of their penance, for, if one went to sleep, they all had to start all over again.

To the west of St. Blane's Chapel is Dunagoil Bay, and on a 50 foot cliff overlooking the bay are the remains of the vitrified fort of Dunagoil. It is a prehistoric fort and it must have been built there to command the lower reaches of the Firth.

We return to Kingarth Church and take the road south again to Kilchattan Bay. This is a small holiday place whose devotees prefer it to the headier charms of Rothesay. The pier has been out of commission for some time, but the Admiralty intend to rebuild it and steamers may be calling there by the time you read this.

The road from Kilchattan Bay back to Rothesay skirts the grounds of Mount Stuart, the home of the Marquis of Bute. The first Mount Stuart House was an 18th century mansion and was burned down in 1877. The magnificent chapel alongside the house was saved. It was a fairly new building, because the third Marquis of Bute had been converted to Roman Catholicism only in 1868. The chapel cost over £100,000 to build. The cost of building it today

Leaving Rothesay on a Clyde Steamer.
Scottish Tourist Board.

would be nearer £1,000,000. Dr. R. Rowand Anderson, an Edinburgh architect, designed the new Mount Stuart House, and it cost £200,000. It is a three-storeyed mansion, and is maybe best described as " a magnificent Gothic structure."

We go by the tree-lined road to the model village of Kerrycroy, designed by one of the Marchionesses of Bute and placed at the entrance gates to Mount Stuart House. Behind these gates a long avenue lined with beech and lime trees leads to the home of the Marquis.

Now we come to Ascog, a village of villas, and to Craig-more, the posh suburb of Rothesay. Craigmore pier, you will see, has been cut off in its prime. The bit that is left is used, when the weather permits, as an open-air café. Once again we pass private hotels, boarding houses, and a hydro perched on the hillside, as we come into the centre of Rothesay.

And from Rothesay pier we get the steamer which is to take us through the most famous scenery in the whole Firth of Clyde—the Kyles of Bute.

P.S. ' Jeanie Deans.'

British Railways.

CHAPTER NINE

THE KYLES OF BUTE

THE most popular of all cruises on the Firth of Clyde is the one to the Kyles of Bute. There are more lively places on the Firth. There are more majestic scenes. But for sheer beauty there is nothing to equal this dog-leg of water running round the Isle of Bute from Rothesay Bay to Ardlamont Point, the promontory between the Kyles and Loch Fyne.

As the steamer sails out from Rothesay pier look straight ahead and see what the weather is like in Loch Striven. It's the long loch that goes straight north from Rothesay and is known as " Rothesay's weatherglass." It's said that, whatever the weather's like in Loch Striven, so it will soon be in Rothesay. In the interests of accuracy I must record that I have seen it pouring in Loch Striven while the whole day has been sunny in Rothesay.

The usual Kyles of Bute cruise doesn't include Loch Striven, but motor boats from Rothesay will take you to see this rather sombre loch. Many years ago Loch Striven was a thriving place and there are said to have been dozens of houses on the west side of the loch, where there is only a very occasional farm now. On the east side a road runs up from Toward and then peters out into a path which joins the main road between Dunoon and Glendaruel near the top of the loch. The Admiralty use Loch Striven for submarine testing, and you will almost certainly see evidence of this at various points in the loch.

As we sail up you see on the right Inverchaolain Church, and, a mile or two farther on, the remains of a pier which was once in regular use. The loch narrows as it reaches the end of its nine mile stretch, and at the top is a big hydro-electric plant.

On the customary cruise we leave Rothesay Bay and cut across Kames Bay, turning into the Kyles of Bute at Ardmaleish Point. We leave Loch Striven on our right and are in the narrows when we pass Strone Point on the mainland. The Isle of Bute is on our left.

If you look at the hill on the right you will perhaps be able to trace some sort of orderly formation in the trees which surround South Hall, the old mansion house on the hillside. These trees were originally planted to represent the formation of the British and French armies at the Battle of Waterloo. The man who built South Hall had fought at Waterloo and conceived this as a memorial. But during the Second World War the Norwegian commandos were trained here, since the area was so like Norway, and their exercises, especially with flame-shooters, burned and blasted the Battle of Waterloo into the few charred relics you see now.

Kyle is the Gaelic word for a narrow strait, and as we approach Colintraive on the right the strait is only about half a mile wide. The mountains rise steeply on the Cowal side, but the hills are gentler on Bute. On the Cowal shore you will see the small, plain Colintraive kirk, and someone aboard the steamer is sure to tell you that the strange thing about the churchyard alongside the kirk is that no one living in Colintraive is allowed to be buried there. When you express surprise, he adds, " They've got to be dead first ! "

Colintraive was to be one of the great holiday places on the Firth at one time, and you'll see a cluster of seven villas built in a much more English than Scottish style, just between the kirk and the ferry. These are known as the " Seven Sisters." They were built when Colintraive was to be " developed," but the great plan was shelved before

Kyles of Bute.

they were completed. The consequence was that the builder had to sell them at a loss.

The car ferry comes out from Colintraive to cross to Rhudabodach on the Bute shore. This is the road link between Rothesay and the mainland. The name Colintraive means " the swimming narrows," and this was where the Highlanders swam their cattle across, going to or from the Isle of Bute. From Colintraive there is a road up the side of Loch Riddon to Glendaruel and thence to Glasgow, Dunoon and Inveraray.

Past Colintraive we come to the Burnt Islands, a group of rocks through which the passage is so narrow that you wonder whether the steamer can make it or not. This is a time when you should go to the bow of the ship, or choose some point of vantage from which you can see what a tight fit it is!

At this point we are turning round the north of Bute. To the right is Loch Riddon but, as in the case of Loch Striven, the customary cruise does not enter the loch.

Near the eastern shore of Loch Riddon is a small island with a single tree growing on it. This is Eilean Dheirg, the Red Island. In 1685 it was fortified by the ninth Earl of Argyll, who had joined in the Duke of Monmouth's rebellion against James II. Argyll landed from Holland at Dunstaffnage in the Highlands and, by sending round the fiery cross, collected some 3,000 men.

His ships attacked the Scottish mainland at various points, but he was always beaten off. At last he sailed into the Kyles of Bute and landed his men and stores on the Red Island. Argyll imagined it was so protected by rocks and the water was so shallow that the Government ships would be unable to attack. He was wrong. Three frigates attacked, the Red Island was taken, and Argyll had to flee. He was captured near Renfrew, taken to Edinburgh and executed there.

The island on the other shore is Eilean Dubh, and you'll see behind it the remains of Glen Caladh Castle. This was a fine house and was inhabited until the Second World War. The Navy took it over and it never recovered. Now Glen Caladh is derelict.

Even if the steamer does cruise up Loch Riddon it can get only half way, for the water becomes too shallow for navigation. Loch Riddon is as charming as Loch Striven is sombre. There is one pier at Ormidale on the western side, but it is not used by steamers. The River Ruel flows into the loch at the top.

On the official cruise we turn through the Burnt Islands and by Glen Caladh to sail south. Over to the left, on the Isle of Bute, you'll see the Maids of Bute. These are two boulders on the hillside painted in red, black and white to resemble two old ladies in Welsh dress. Nobody knows why this was first done, nor by whom. But the painting is kept up to this day, though this part of Bute is wild and uninhabited.

We sail down to Tighnabruaich, Gaelic for " the house on the brae." The name comes from an inn which once stood on the hillside. Tighnabruaich is a most charming place with a pier, tea rooms, hotels and—surprising in a village so remote—a cinema. This is the end of the usual cruise, and time is allowed on shore.

Some steamers sail on right down the Kyles and into the Sound of Bute. There are two piers farther down on the mainland side. The first is Auchenlochan and the second Kames, but neither is used now. A clachan clusters round each pier, and these places are also holiday centres, though smaller than Tighnabruaich. These pleasant resorts have only one drawback. The midges, as they say in these parts, have clogs on! The shops in Tighnabruaich will sell you protective ointments.

The road that runs up the hill from Kames is the one which joins the main road up Loch Fyneside. This is the Ardlamont peninsula between the Kyles of Bute and Loch Fyne.

The Kyles begin to widen as we sail down between the Ardlamont land and the Isle of Bute. On Bute we see farms, houses and cultivated land instead of heather and rocks. The island straight ahead of us in Inch Marnock, the " Drunkard's Isle." In the background to the south are the towering peaks of Arran.

As its name suggests, Ardlamont was the ground belonging to the Clan Lamont and their chieftain lived in Ardlamont House. As we are leaving the Kyles of Bute we see the grounds of Ardlamont House, though to see the house itself we must go round Ardlamont Point and into Loch Fyne.

Ardlamont House was the scene of one of Scotland's most renowned murder cases, the " Ardlamont Mystery." In 1893 a well-dressed, glibly spoken gentleman named A. J. Monson took over the house and installed his wife, family and pupil there. His pupil was a young man named Windsor Dudley Cecil Hambrough. Monson was a confidence trickster of considerable experience, and he hoodwinked the people of the district completely. His carriage would carry him to Kames pier so that he could join the steamer to go up to Glasgow on business.

His business was to insure his pupil. When he did get
an insurance policy fixed, he and a " civil engineer " who
suddenly arrived on the scene took young Hambrough
out fishing one night in Ardlamont Bay. There was a
hole in the bottom of the boat and it sank while Monson
and Hambrough were in it. But both swam safely to the
shore.

Early next morning they took Hambrough out shooting.
After a while Monson came back to Ardlamont House with
the news that Hambrough had accidentally shot himself
while climbing over a fence. He then claimed the insurance.

But the insurance company and the police were not
satisfied. The " civil engineer " disappeared and Monson
was taken to the High Court in Edinburgh and charged
with murdering his pupil. The jury found the case against
him " Not Proven," that peculiarly Scottish verdict which
means, according to the cynics, " Go away and don't do it
again!" Monson went away and was involved in various
other shady incidents. He served several terms in prison
and was eventually killed in a brawl in a diamond mine
district in South Africa.

Looking at Ardlamont from the sea, you'll agree that
there could hardly be a more unsuitable background for
such a macabre story. The Ardlamont mystery ranks along
with the Goatfell murder (I tell the story in my chapter on
Arran) as the two great murder cases of the Firth of Clyde.

Now we have sailed through the Kyles of Bute. We've
come from Rothesay on the east coast of Bute to Ettrick
Bay on the west. We've traversed the northern half of the
island and have travelled 15 miles by water. Yet the land
distance between Ettrick Bay and Rothesay is only three
miles.

Once more we leave the Highland side of the Firth of
Clyde and cross the water to the Lowland shore, to the
golden coasts of Ayrshire.

CHAPTER TEN

THE GOLF COAST

COMING down the Lowland side of the Firth of Clyde we stopped at Portencross Castle. Now we complete this part of the Firth by following the Golf Coast from West Kilbride to Ayr. I call it the Golf Coast because, between these two towns in Ayrshire, there are 20 golf courses. That's an average of one per mile!

Among them are some of the finest golf courses in the world—two of them championship links. But not one is a poor course, for Ayrshire seems almost to have been specially designed by Providence for the playing of golf. There are no mountains, not even very many hills. Many of the courses are made by the side of the sea and have magnificent views over to the Isle of Arran. As I've said, golf is a very democratic game in Scotland, probably more so than in any other country in the world, including England. It is also cheaper to play here than anywhere else.

Don't think, though, that Ayrshire is famous only for golf. It is the birthplace of Robert Burns and almost everywhere you go has some Burns connection. It is the land of the original Old King Cole. Just as King Arthur was supposed to have lived around Dumbarton, so Old King Cole is said to have held his court in the part of Ayrshire we call Kyle. Robert Burns called it Coil, so the merry old soul should really be Auld King Coil.

The three ports of this part of Ayrshire are Ardrossan, Troon and Ayr. There are cruises touching all three, but owing to the deep bays of Ayr and Irvine, the steamer is too far from land for you to see anything clearly without the aid of field glasses. So rather than tell you what you see from the sea, I'll describe the Golf Coast from the landsman's point of view. Ayrshire is well served by roads and railways, and is very popular with holiday-makers.

The first golf course in this 20 miles is West Kilbride and we see it as we leave Portencross Castle and come round Farland Head. West Kilbride itself is set on a hill a mile or so inland. Although it's regarded as a seaside resort, it's quite a distance from any beach. The nearest is the suburb of Seamill. At the Seamill Hydro football teams sometimes train, and the famous Celtic club of Glasgow used the hydro for many years.

The road runs close to the sea all the way to Ardrossan, and there are caravan sites and bathing beaches. Out from Ardrossan you can see Horse Island, to which the local " cowboys " sometimes swim cattle. It is occasionally used for grazing during the summer, but is mostly inhabited by sea birds.

Ardrossan is a comparatively modern town and is the port for ships to Arran, Ireland and the Isle of Man. The Earls of Eglinton hoped to develop it industrially and one of them planned a canal from Glasgow to Ardrossan. It got only as far as Paisley. Another Earl built the harbour. The railways came in and built piers and sidings. The main part of the town was laid out in rectangular style about 1806.

Just by Ardrossan station are the ruins of Ardrossan Castle. It was captured by Sir William Wallace (who did many of his most valiant deeds hereabouts) from the English. But Cromwell came along a few hundred years later and destroyed it, as was his wont!

Ardrossan stretches round South Bay to join the holiday resort of Saltcoats. This beach is popular with day trippers from Glasgow, and you can hardly see it in summer without its quota of church outings, bus parties, and children's excursions. Saltcoats is much older than Ardrossan. James the Fifth established a saltworks here in the 16th century and that's how Saltcoats got its name. Tourism is now its principal industry and it has a summer theatre, a bathing pool and a harbour which is used mainly for pleasure cruise motor boats.

The road leads inland from Saltcoats to Stevenston and takes a wide curve round by Kilwinning, back to Irvine on the coast. This is because nearly four miles of the coastline and a great area behind that are occupied by the Ardeer Works of the Imperial Chemical Industries. Among other things, they make high explosives, and the works were started by the same Nobel who gave the Peace Prize to the world. The place is so immense that visitors are shown round by bus.

Kilwinning is a pleasant little town and is famous for the fact that freemasonry in Scotland was started here. When Kilwinning Priory (now no more) was built in the 12th century, some of the foreign workers are said to have introduced freemasonry, and a plain, unassuming building on the main street proclaims itself " Mother Lodge Kilwinning." It is the parent lodge of the craft in Scotland.

The road to Irvine runs alongside the wall of Eglinton Castle grounds. The castle was used as a hospital during the war. It was built at the end of the 18th century and is noted for the great Eglinton Tournament held there in 1839. This was an attempt to re-create the days of chivalry. The " Queen of Beauty " was Lady Seymour, a granddaughter of Sheridan, and one of the knights was Napoleon III.

Bogside Racecourse is on the right as you come into the Royal Burgh of Irvine by way of the Town Moor. Irvine was made a Royal Burgh in the 13th century and it runs the oldest horse race in the world. The organisation in charge is a secret society, the Irvine Carters. When the Marymass races are held in August, the big event is for horses owned by Brother Carters, and it's an amazing sight to see great Clydesdales thundering down the course, with the jockeys bouncing about on the broad backs and clods of earth flying from the huge feet. Despite the mechanisation of farming, this famous race is as popular as ever.

Irvine is one of the oldest ports on the Firth of Clyde, but it is known today as a go-ahead industrial centre. Among its many industries maybe the most unusual is making prefabricated huts for African natives.

John Galt, the novelist, was born in Irvine in 1771. Edgar Allan Poe lived in the town when he was a boy. Robert Burns came to Irvine to learn the art of flax-dressing, but the first Hogmanay he was there the New Year celebrations were so intense that the shop was burned down. Just off the main street the site of the house where he lived in 1781, is marked by a plaque. There is a fine statue of Burns by the side of the River Irvine, in front of Irvine Academy.

Every year, as a climax to Marymass Week, the Marymass Queen is crowned in front of the Town Hall after the Irvine Carters and their supporters on horseback have ridden round the bounds of the town. Then there is a procession through the streets to the Town Moor for the Marymass Races.

Irvine is one of the places in Scotland which preserve the old trade guilds, and the Trades meet every year for the " Big Pie." This annual dinner commemorates the time when the whole repast was one huge pie into which all the diners dipped as they felt inclined. Nowadays individual pies are served!

Although Irvine is not reckoned as a holiday resort, it has one of the finest beaches in Ayrshire. Apart from a vestigial promenade and a tea room, it has not been developed. Unfortunately it is backed at first by works and then by a shooting range. It's possible, however, to walk along the sands to Barassie and Troon, over four miles.

The road is some distance inland and is separated from the sea by the railway and golf courses. The track which crosses under the road runs between Kilmarnock and Troon and was the first railway to be made in Scotland.

About three miles towards Kilmarnock (a town which has the distinction of being regarded as the best balanced industrially in this country) is Dundonald, where you see the ruins of Dundonald Castle. This was Robert the Second's home before he became King of Scotland, and he died here in 1390. James Boswell took Dr. Sam Johnson to see it in 1773 and the sage " was very jocular on the homely accommodation of King Bob, and roared and laughed till the ruins echoed."

We get back on to the sea-front at Barassie, a dormitory suburb of Troon with a fine golf course and what seems the largest proportion of television aerials to houses in these parts.

Now we are at Troon, the town which leads a double life. A nose of land pokes out into the Firth, dividing Irvine Bay from Ayr Bay. It also divides industrial Troon from holiday Troon. At the harbour there is a thriving shipyard and a shipbreaking yard, and all the industrial paraphernalia required to keep a busy port going. But if you are on holiday in Troon, you see nothing of this—unless you sail from the harbour on one of the steamer cruises.

Holiday Troon has sands and links and hotels and a bathing pool which vies with the Prestwick Bathing Lake farther along the coast. Troon has six golf courses, including the famous championship one.

Out in the Firth a mile and a half from Troon is Lady Isle, a rock with a light and a small house on it. Lady Isle is a bird sanctuary and is leased by the Portland Estates to the Society for the Protection of Wild Birds at a rent of half-a-crown a year. During the summer a bird watcher sometimes lives in the house and presents a report to the Society at the end of his lonely vigil.

Once again the road goes inland and leaves the shore to the railway and the golf courses. We come into Prestwick by the village of Monkton, which has the ruins of an ancient kirk and a monument to James Macrae, the poor Ayrshire boy who became Governor of Madras in the 18th century. Most visitors hardly notice Monkton because they are on the edge of one of the world's international airports, Prestwick.

Prestwick is the only fog-free airport in the British Isles, and is often used as an alternative to London and other English airports. It has direct air services to all parts of the world, including the United States of America, Holland, France, Canada, Eire, Switzerland, Denmark, Sweden, Germany and Finland.

Before the Second World War, a training school for R.A.F. pilots was started here and when the war began it became the Headquarters of R.A.F. Ferry Command. The first Transatlantic plane came in on November 29, 1940, and before the war was over some 40,000 Transatlantic planes had landed here. From 1943 to 1945 it was the main centre for the U.S. Transport Command, and it was also the chief Transit Evacuation Hospital between France and the U.S.A.

Prestwick is not simply a civilian airport. It is also an American Air Base and it contains the considerable works of Scottish Aviation, Ltd. Scottish Aviation's main building, by the way, is one of the big pavilions from the Empire Exhibition of 1938 held in Glasgow.

Control Tower, Prestwick Airport.

The airport buildings themselves are erected around Orangefield House, a mansion which Robert Burns visited. You can see a line of his verse above the original door —"A pleasant spot near sandy wilds." The Airport Restaurant is well worth visiting, for travellers are coming in constantly from all parts of the world. You can tell where they are from, because the appropriate national flag is placed on each table. The restaurant is an excellent one.

Prestwick is a thriving holiday centre. The village had its origins in Robert the Bruce's day, but now it is an up-to-date town with many hotels, a long promenade and a Bathing Lake with accommodation for 1,200 bathers and nearly a million gallons of water. This in spite of the fact that there are good bathing beaches on either side of it.

There are coal-mines behind Prestwick and the workings extend two miles out under the sea. A number of the miners are members of the Prestwick Swimming Club, so they work under the Lake during the day and come along in the evening to swim over the top of their work!

Only two remnants of historical Prestwick are left. One is the old Mercat Cross in the middle of the town. The other is on the main road out of Prestwick to Ayr. In an open space on the right, by the Episcopal church, is the Kingcase Well. Here Robert the Bruce is supposed to have been cured of a skin disease.

Prestwick, Newton-on-Ayr and Ayr are now one solid line of buildings and it's difficult to tell which is which. Seen from the sea, it's not just difficult, it's impossible.

Ayr is a fine county town with a population moving to the 50,000 mark. It is a hunting centre, a port, a holiday resort and the heart of the Burns Country. In the summer the population of Ayr goes up to well over 100,000, many of them Glaswegians who make the main street look just like Argyle Street on a Saturday night! There are golf courses, a racecourse, cinemas, dance halls, an ice rink, and two theatres, including the famous Gaiety run by the Popplewell brothers. Their father is said to have been the original of the summer show proprietor in J. B. Priestley's " Good Companions."

The customary Ayrshire holiday pattern of long links and great beaches of golden sand is followed here. A promenade extends from the harbour to the River Doon, and there are putting greens, a fun fair and gardens along it.

Ayr is a very old town, but there are not many signs of its antiquity. William the Lion granted Ayr its charter as a

Ayr.   Scottish Tourist Board.

Royal Burgh in 1202, and right in the middle of the town
is the Auld Brig, crossing the River Ayr, which is said to
be nearly as old as that charter. It has not been definitely
proved that it's a 13th century structure, though it's un-
deniably very old indeed.

It is the same Auld Brig mentioned in Robert Burns'
poem, " The Brigs of Ayr." For hundreds of years it was
the only bridge in the town, though you can see how right
Burns was when he described it as a " poor narrow footpath of a street, where twa wheelbarrows tremble when
they meet." In the poem the two bridges address each
other, and to the New Brig's scornful words the Auld
Brig retorts, " I'll be a brig when ye're a shapeless cairn."
This was a remarkable prophecy by Burns. Just under
100 years after Burns wrote these words, the New Brig
was so damaged by floods that it collapsed. The present
New Brig is the second bridge there, and it was built in 1879.

The Auld Brig was condemned by the authorities at the
beginning of this century. Burns Clubs all over Britain
immediately rallied their members to the support of the
ancient bridge. The public interest was aroused and
enough money came in to allow the Auld Brig to be
strengthened and repaired. Lord Rosebery, on behalf of
the Burns Federation, performed the reopening ceremony
in 1910. All that remains of the original New Brig is a
group of statuary in the grounds of Burns's Cottage at
Alloway.

If you go from the Auld Brig into the High Street you
will see the narrow Kirk Port which leads to Ayr Old Parish
Church, built in 1655. The money for building it was
actually given by Cromwell to recompense the town for the
mess he had made of the 12th century church of St. John,
which he had converted into an armoury. There are
some interesting memorials of Ayr in the Parish Church,
including the tattered colours of the North British Fusiliers.
In the kirkyard there are ancient stones and monuments,
and the outstanding one is the Martyrs' Monument, on
which the inscription tells the story:—

> Here lie seven Martyrs for our Covenant,
> A sacred number of triumphant Saints,
> Pontius McAdam the unjust sentence past,
> What is his own the world will know at last!
> And Herod Drummond caused their heads affix,
> Heaven keep a record of the sixty-six,
> Boots, thumbkins, gibbets were in fashion then.
> Lord, let us never see such Days again.

If you go back down the Kirk Port to the High Street and continue south, you come to the Wallace Tower. A statue of Sir William Wallace by James Thom, the Ayrshire sculptor whose figures of Tam o' Shanter and Souter Johnny are so well known, stands half way up the 113-foot tower. Some people in Ayr will tell you that Wallace was imprisoned in that very tower, and others that the tower is built on the site of an older one in which Wallace was imprisoned. But the present Wallace Tower was built in 1834, and the original Tower was a seat of the Cathcart family, and not turned into a prison until 1673. Wallace, may I remind you, lived in the 13th century. His principal exploit hereabouts was the burning of the " Barns of Ayr." These " barns " were barracks in which the English troops were quartered.

Not far along the High Street from the Wallace Tower is the Tam o' Shanter Inn, now a Burns museum. This is supposed to be the inn where Tam o' Shanter started his journey and inspired what many people regard as Burns' greatest poem. In 1943 the Inn was threatened with demolition but Ayr Burns Club raised £1,250 towards the cost of buying it, and the town eventually paid £4,000 for it. Some experts say, however, that it has nothing to do with Burns and didn't even exist in the poet's day.

Before we concentrate on the man who wrote in that same poem—

> Auld Ayr, wham ne'er a town surpasses
> For honest men and bonnie lasses,

we'll look at the rest of the Royal Burgh.

The Harbour of Ayr is said to be the oldest in the West

f Scotland, and it is believed that it was a harbour in the days when King Haakon was beaten at the Battle of Largs 1263). It is used mainly by coal boats and fishing smacks, nd there are pleasure cruises throughout the summer from Ayr to various parts of the Firth, particularly the Isle of Arran, straight across the water. It was from this port that Edward Bruce sailed with his army in 1315 to invade Ireland.

To the south from Ayr Harbour stands Loudon Hall, a 16th century building which has been restored. Near it in Fort Street is Ayr Academy. It was founded in 1233. By Cromwell Place you get to Fort Castle and you can climb to the top of the 12th century tower of the Church of St. John the Baptist, the one which Cromwell turned into an armoury. The Fort was built in the grounds round he church in 1652. In this church the Scottish Parliament met in 1315 to settle the succession of the Scottish crown n the event of the death of King Robert the Bruce.

Not far from the tower is Wellington Place, a fine square with mansions turned into hotels and offices on two sides, and the imposing County Buildings at the seaward end. Among the monuments here are the War Memorial and he statue of John Loudon Macadam, the 19th century roadmaker from Ayr who gave his name to " macadam-sing " streets and roads.

You may go to Ayr for all sorts of reasons but, whatever your purpose, the one thing you can't escape is the influence of Robert Burns. The whole world knows this Scottish farmer poet. I've heard his words quoted by Russians in Moscow and by a Filipino waiter in Ch'cago. Visitors come from every country to see the Burns Country, and Ayr is its natural centre.

Supposing we follow the imaginary journey of Tam o' Shanter from Ayr to the Brig o' Doon. We go back to the Tam o' Shanter Inn in the High Street, and there—

Ae market night,
Tam had got planted unco right,
Fast by an ingle, bleezing finely,
Wi' reaming swats that drank divinely . . .

Now, as I've said, the inn is a museum, but you will be shown the very kitchen where Thomas Graham of Shanter (Tam's proper name) sat with his old crony, Souter Johnny. Then, despite the storm, he decided to ride home on his grey mare Meg.

We can't follow Tam o' Shanter's exact route, because the old road south was a winding one, and it's a pretty straight main thoroughfare now. You leave the Tam o' Shanter Inn and walk along Alloway Street to Burns Statue Square. The main feature of the square is the statue of Robert Burns, who is looking towards his birthplace at Alloway. His view is now circumscribed by a cinema and the Ayr Ice Rink. From this square you can get a bus to Burns's Cottage, Alloway Kirk and the Burns Monument at Brig o' Doon. The total distance is only two and a quarter miles.

We go out Monument Road and have just left Ayr when we come to the bridge over the Slaphouse Burn. About 200 yards on to the left was . . .

> the ford,
> Where in the snaw the chapman smoor'd.

Just under 100 yards on the right we come to a cottage garden where once stood . . .

> the meikle stane,
> Where drunken Charlie brak's neck-bane.

On the same side of the road is beautiful Belleisle Park, belonging to the town of Ayr. Next we come to the auld clay biggin' where Burns was born but, since he doesn't mention it in " Tam o' Shanter," we'll go straight on after Tam and return to his author later. Just past the Cottage on the right is Cambusdoon. In the park is an ash tree surrounded by a railing. This is where Tam saw . . .

> the cairn,
> Where hunters fand the murder'd bairn.

As you can see, the road which Tam and Meg took was much more to the west than the one you are travelling on, so that

the well,
> Where Mungo's mither hang'd hersel

is actually 200 yards from the main road, down a footpath
along the River Doon, and you see " Kirk Alloway . . .
where ghaists and hoolets nightly cry " before you see the
site of the well.

Even in bright sunlight the ruin of Alloway Kirk has a
sinister look—especially if you have read " Tam o' Shanter "
just before setting out on this pilgrimage. With a little
trouble you can look through the window which Tam
looked through, and you're gazing directly at

> the winnock bunker in the east,
> Where sat Auld Nick in shape o' beast.

This is where Tam " saw an unco sight," and I get a
chill down the spine every time I look through that window.

The grave of Burns's father, William Burnes, is just at the
entrance to the kirkyard. His wife is also mentioned on the
tombstone, but she is not buried there. This, by the way,
is not the original tombstone. It was chipped into fragments
by souvenir hunters.

And now Tam o' Shanter has seen the wild dance of
witches and, ere he can help himself, has roared out,
" Weel done, Cutty Sark!" And in a moment all was dark,
and out the hellish legion sall'ed after Tam and his
grey mare Meg. Tam knew he must cross running water to
be free of the witches, but Cutty Sark was leading the
crew just behind him. We can take his way, across from
the kirk and down the lane between the Burns Monument
Hotel and the Grecian outline of the Monument. Then we
climb to the ancient bridge over the River Doon.

It's very easy to imagine the " Tam o' Shanter " scene
here. The Brig o' Doon is a tall, slender arch and you
can get to the key-stane o' the brig where Meg gave one
bound forward and rescued her master, but left her tail
in the clutch of Cutty Sark.

May I remind visitors, and especially our American
friends, that the Brig o' Doon has nothing whatever to do
with the musical play, " Brigadoon." The only point of

Burns Cottage, Alloway. Scottish Tourist Board.

contact is the name itself. There is no disappearing village of Brigadoon here.

You can visit the Banks o' Doon Tea Gardens, right down by ye banks and braes o' bonnie Doon, and you can also visit the Burns Monument. The Monument was built in 1820 and it is a museum as well as a memorial. Among the exhibits are Jean Armour's wedding ring, and the Bible with which Burns " married " Highland Mary across running water. (As you can see, running water has all sorts of uses in Scotland!) In a grotto near the Monument are the life-size statues of Tam o' Shanter and Souter Johnny made by James Thom.

Now we retrace our steps to the Mecca of all Burns lovers, the auld clay biggin' where Burns was born. From the main road you're really looking at the back of the cottage. The original road ran on the other side of the building. William Burnes built this but and ben himself and on January 25, 1759, Robert Burns was born there. The wind blew the thatched roof off one night, but William Burnes replaced it and Robert spent the first seven years of his life there.

Robert's father ran a market garden, but gave it up to farm at Mount Oliphant, about two miles away. He kept the property, however, and sold it in 1781 to the Incorporation of Shoemakers in Ayr for £160. By the year 1800 it had been turned into an ale-house. Robert Burns died in Dumfries on July 21, 1796, and some ten years later people started to flock to see the place where he was born. The Ayr Shoemakers cashed in on this, and added outhouses to sell more ale to the visitors.

Royal visit to birthplace of Robert Burns.

Scottish Tourist Board.

Meanwhile the Burns Monument had been built and the trustees were very worried that the birthplace of the poet should be a pub. By charging twopence to visitors to the Monument they raised enough money to buy the Cottage from the Shoemakers in 1881. It cost them £4,000, and then they spent more money on returning the Cottage to more or less its original form and developing the five acres of ground behind it into a garden. They also built a Burns Museum alongside the Cottage, and today it houses the greatest collection of Burnsiana in the world.

On an average 100,000 people visit Burns's Cottage every year. The octogenarian curator, Thomas MacMynn, has shown round such visitors as Queen Elizabeth, Malenkov, Clark Gable, Dr. Wellington Koo, Irving Berlin, the Duke of Windsor, and Joe Louis. Mr. MacMynn can recite by heart every poem and song that Robert Burns wrote. He can also recite every important published letter by Burns.

The Cottage is very plain. You enter by the byre and stables, and you see the ben before the but! The but is the kitchen, and the ben is the parlour, and an invitation to " come ben the hoose " is to go from the kitchen into the " good " room. Some relics of Robert Burns are kept in the Cottage, but all the really valuable material is in the Museum across the garden. This Museum has thousands of relics of Robert Burns and his friends, and books by and about Burns. There are original manuscripts, first editions, busts of the poet, brooches, seals, spoons, punch-bowls, clocks, panes of glass with poetry written with a diamond by Burns, walking sticks, stained glass windows, letters, razors, paintings, snuff boxes, and a lock of Burns's hair.

Although it's not strictly the Firth of Clyde, the hinter-land of Burns's Cottage should be mentioned. From Ayr you can get easily by bus to a great many places associated with the poet.

From the Cottage it's only two miles to Mount Oliphant, now a thriving farm. It was here that Robert, at the age of

14, wrote his first poem. It was dedicated to a girl who worked beside him in the harvest field and was entitled " My Handsome Nell."

There is a direct road from Ayr to Mauchline, and about half way along it you can take a side road to the north and Tarbolton; Burns lived at Lochlea Farm, about three miles out of Tarbolton, from his 17th to his 24th year. He founded the Bachelor's Club in Tarbolton and it is now a Burns museum. Among other poems, he wrote ' Death and Dr. Hornbook " here.

Back on the main road you'll go by Montgomerie Estate, where Burns may have met Highland Mary. You come to Failford, with its quaint wee inn and a monument on the bank of the Fail Burn marking the spot where Burns and Highland Mary met " to live one day of parting love."

Mauchline has many memories of Robert Burns. There is Poosie Nansie's Inn, the scene of " The Jolly Beggars." Beside it is the site of Nance Tinnock's alehouse. Opposite is Mauchline kirkyard in which many of the Burns characters are buried—including the infamous " Holy Willie." Near-by is the house where Burns took Jean Armour to live. By this time you won't be surprised to know that it's now a museum.

Just outside Mauchline are the National Burns Memorial and Cottage Homes. The Memorial is a tower, and also a museum. From the top you can see the farm of Mossgiel, where Burns lived from 1784 to 1788, and where he wrote " The Cottar's Saturday Night," " Hallowe'en," " Holy Willie's Prayer," " The Twa Dogs," " Address to the Unco Guid," " To a Mountain Daisy," and " The Jolly Beggars."

The strange thing about Robert Burns was that he lived for most of his life within sight of the amazing mountain silhouette of the Isle of Arran. He must have seen it day after day, yet he never mentioned it in any of his poems.

But all the way down the Golf Coast we have seen it. And now is the time to cross the Firth of Clyde to this most enchanting of all islands.

CHAPTER ELEVEN

THE
EPITOME
OF
SCOTLAND

THE Isle of Arran has been called " the epitome of Scotland " because every kind of scenery in our country can be seen in this island, which is less than 60 miles round by road. Geologists use the same term because Arran is a geological freak, and possesses almost every type of geological formation known in Britain. Climbers think Arran is wonderful because the climbing in the ' Arran Alps ' is as varied as you'll find in Scotland.

Arran has a population of between 4,500 and 5,000, and it is estimated that there are now as many deer as people on the island, which is the largest in the Firth of Clyde. Once it was a completely Highland island, but now only a few of the old people have the Gaelic, a special sort of Arran Gaelic.

According to Celtic literature, Arran was the favourite island of the great hero, Fingal, and his friends. There are many Ossianic legends connected with various parts of Arran, particularly in the south, the part nearest Ireland.

The Vikings occupied it.   Then it was a royal hunting domain of the Scottish kings.   The English took it over and were turned out by Bruce's men.   Cromwell settled a garrison on the island and they were all killed.   In time most of Arran came into the possession of the ducal family of Hamilton, and the last laird was the Duchess of Montrose, whose death meant that the lands had to be sold to pay the death duties.

For something like 100 years Arran has been a great holiday centre, but not in the popular sense.   Arran offers bathing, fishing, golf, tennis, bowling, climbing, walking, boating and all the natural country sports.   But it has none of the amenities deemed desirable in holiday resorts like Largs, Rothesay and Dunoon—to say nothing of Brighton, Bournemouth, Blackpool and the like.

In the summer the three villages on the east side— Brodick, Lamlash and Whiting Bay—have a cinema show twice a week, and there is usually a weekly show in Lochranza and Kilmory.   But the only other sophisticated entertainments are dancing and occasional performances by local amateur drama groups.   Arran preserves a completely country atmosphere and that is why it attracts its regular followers, people who have been going to the one place in Arran for generations.   Arran exercises a hypnotic effect on many West of Scotland people, and perhaps I should confess that this year I have already been in Arran eight times, and there are still two months to go!

The usual way to go to Arran is by steamer or car ferry from Ardrossan in the summer and Fairlie in the winter. But many cruises touch at Arran and the regular summer service to Campbeltown calls in at Lochranza pier. The voyage takes about an hour and the great thrill is to stand on the steamer deck and see the amazing Wagnerian backdrop of the Arran mountains come nearer and nearer. All the mountains are in the north of the island and the ground slopes down towards Lamlash, with its conical Holy Isle in front of it, and then becomes undulating hills until it reaches the long, golden beaches in the south.

From the deck you see the renowned " Sleeping Warrior."
This is an outline of mountains which gives the effect of a
knight in armour recumbent, as seen in many a church
memorial. Superior people are inclined to laugh at this
conceit, but ordinary holiday-makers enjoy the illusion
and point it out excitedly to each other.

We sail into the delightful Brodick Bay, with its sweep
of golden beach and brightly-painted bathing boxes, its
line of hotels, trees, golf courses, hills, and then the mighty
Goatfell, with the pink Brodick Castle in the woods beneath
it. Brodick is the capital of Arran and the chief port. In
winter Brodick is the only port.

Devoted Arranites are apt to look down on Brodick
because it is the natural place for the day trippers to stay in.
Just behind the pier are lines of buses ready to take you
anywhere on the island, or right round the island if you've
a mind to tour. Most " Round the Island " buses make the
tour counter-clockwise, so we shall follow their example.

Brodick was originally a clachan called Invercloy, and
the first Brodick was near the Castle. But from the pier to
the Castle it's all Brodick now. There is a line of hotels to
the shopping centre, but maybe I'd better point out that the
shopping centre has only seven or eight shops! Here is the
beach, the putting green, tea rooms and the public hall.
This is the metropolis of Arran, so you can imagine what
the other places are like—though I should add that Lamlash
and Whiting Bay can compete in the number of shops.

Opposite the golf clubhouse a road goes up to Kilmichael
House. It's now a private hotel but it was once the seat of
the Fullartons—for long the only landowners of Arran
apart from the Hamilton family. The first Fullarton fought
valiantly for Robert the Bruce in his war for Scottish
independence, and the King later granted him this piece
of land in Arran. The Fullarton family are still represented
in Brodick, but most of the land is no longer theirs.

We follow the road round towards Brodick Castle. In
front of Brodick School there is a statue to the 11th Duke
of Hamilton, who was much beloved by his tenants. On

the right of the road is a Druid's stone, one of the many ancient remains to be found on Arran. It is now used for posting notices of concerts and dances.

The road which leads to the left past the Druid's stone is the String Road, one of two which cross the island. It's so called because, to mariners out in the Firth, it looks just like a piece of string laid across the hill. This is the way you take to Glen Rosa, a wonderful natural beauty spot, to Glen Sheraig, and to the Shiskine valley and Blackwaterfoot. When you go up the String Road, the first path to the right is the one for the two glens.

Around here, as in most parts of Arran, there is a deal of fairy lore. Arran has fairies of its own. There are three kinds of fairy—the brownies, the bocans and the bleaters. The brownies are the traditional " little folk," and in many farmhouses a dish of milk is left out at night for them to sup. The bocans are big, tough, nasty fairies and do harm

Arran: Glen Rosa.

to people. The bleaters come drifting into your houses at night and sit by the fire and weep. They are the Arran equivalent of zombies.

Not long ago a holiday-maker who was boarding at a farm in Glen Sheraig was warned by his host not to go out walking late at night. The visitor paid no attention to this warning and about 2 a.m., when he found he wasn't sleeping well, he decided to go for a walk up the String Road. He rose and dressed and climbed the hill. When he reached the first bridge on the other side he looked down at the burn beneath. In the shade of the trees he saw a man standing, so he shouted a greeting. The figure raised its arms as if it held a bow and arrow, and suddenly the visitor felt such a violent pain in his leg that he fainted.

When he regained consciousness, it was broad daylight. His leg was still sore but he could see no mark on it. He hobbled back to the farm in Glen Sheraig and confessed to the farmer what had happened. " Ah, yes," nodded the farmer instantly, " that would be an elf-shot."

We leave the String Road and continue round by the bounds of Brodick Castle estate. Brodick Castle now belongs to the National Trust for Scotland. There was a danger when the Duchess of Montrose died that it would be sold as a hotel or rendered roofless, but the National Trust made a public appeal for funds which was answered in record time. Lady Jean Fforde, daughter of the Duchess, also offered the mountain of Goatfell to the nation and this was accepted.

The customary way up Goatfell is clearly marked. You go through the estate into a wood and then reach a path. Goatfell (the name has nothing to do with goats— it's derived from the Gaelic and means " mountain of the winds ") is 2,866 feet high and is the highest of Arran mountains. These mountains seem even bigger than they are because you see them from sea level, which is unusual in the case of most mountains. You should allow three hours to climb Goatfell and two hours to come down. It can be done quicker than this, but five hours are just about right if you are going to enjoy yourself. In the annual Goatfell Race, held during Arran Week in June, cross-country runners do the journey from Brodick Post Office to the summit and back in about one and a quarter hours.

The walk up is not too strenuous until you reach the last 200 feet. Don't attempt to go straight up the mountain. Keep to the ridge on the right. The final 200 feet means using your hands as well as your feet. It's a bit of a scramble and not recommended to anyone suffering from vertigo. The view from the top is immense. On a clear day you can see 126 mountains. The whole Firth of Clyde is spread out before you, and you can even see the Hebrides.

This is the place where the victim of the Goatfell Murder was last seen, on the evening of July 15, 1889. He was Edwin Robert Rose, a young London clerk on holiday, and he had climbed the mountain with a dark, saturnine Scotsman named John Watson Laurie, whom he'd met at Rothesay. They had come to Brodick so that they could climb Goatfell.

About 10 o'clock that night Laurie was seen near the Sannox burying ground and then in the bar of Corrie Hotel. He left Brodick early next morning. A week or so later Rose's family in London became worried at the non-appearance of Edwin and started making enquiries. Search parties were organised in Arran and on August 4 one of the searchers found Rose's body concealed under a huge boulder in the Corrie of Fire, not far down from the summit of Goatfell. He had suffered head injuries and his money and return ticket to London were missing.

Meanwhile Laurie had disappeared. From various places he wrote letters to the newspapers denying that he had murdered Rose. On September 3 he was caught near Larkhall in Lanarkshire, and he was tried for the murder of Rose in November. The Edinburgh jury found him guilty and he was sentenced to death. This sentence was commuted to penal servitude for life, and he spent the next 41 years in prison. He died in Perth Prison on October 4, 1930.

There are people today who hold that Laurie was not guilty of murder, though he was guilty of robbing Rose. They think that Rose slipped as he came down the mountainside and that Laurie panicked and hid the body. Nobody will ever know the truth.

We come down the mountain and keep by the wall of Brodick Castle, which is now open to the public and is well worth visiting. It's believed that there was a Viking fort here in the days when the Norwegians ruled these waves. There was a castle when the Macdonalds of the Isles held Arran. Then in 1306 Brodick Castle fell to the English, until they were driven out by Bruce's men led by the Black Douglas. You can see Bruce's table and Bruce's room in Brodick Castle today.

It had all the ups and downs of Scottish historical castles, so only a small part of it is ancient. The rest, built in the Scottish Baronial style, is fairly new. The principal rooms are open to the public and there is a priceless collection of paintings, silver and objets-d'art.

You can also see Brodick Castle Gardens, which were the special care of the Duchess of Montrose and are now owned by the National Trust for Scotland. Here is a collection of sub-tropical plants, rhododendrons and exotic trees, regarded by experts as one of the finest in Europe.

Rhododendrons line our route as we go by the coast road round to Corrie, six miles north of Brodick. Corrie is a charming village a mile long and popular with mountaineers who can get into the hills faster from this vantage point. It's also popular with artists, and probably more pictures have been painted of Corrie and High Corrie than any other part of Arran. High Corrie is a tiny clachan perched on the hill above Corrie and as many as 16 artists have been seen sitting round it, painting for all they were worth!

Even higher than High Corrie is Upper High Corrie and here you'll see the stones among the heather that mark where a village once stood. The grandfather of Prime Minister Harold Macmillan lived here for a while, although the family lived originally near Lochranza.

The sea front, Corrie.

Once you could stand at the very bar window where Laurie stood after the murder, but the hotel has been considerably changed. It was a Corrie policeman who figured in one of the sensational incidents of the trial, when counsel for the defence kept asking the police to produce Rose's boots. At last this policeman admitted that he had buried them on the Corrie beach below the low water mark, because there was a superstition in Arran that a murdered man's ghost would walk if his boots weren't buried.

A mile beyond Corrie is Sannox, and it's in Sannox graveyard that Rose now lies. His grave is marked by a big boulder.

Near the Sannox beach is the southern mark of the Measured Mile off Arran. Here the liners and warships carry out their tests, because their wash would interfere with steamer and other traffic if they used the Measured Mile at Skelmorlie. Along that beach you can reach the

Fallen Rocks, a mass of tumbled boulders resulting from a cliff fall over 200 years ago.

But we keep to the road and now we start climbing by Glen Sannox and North Glen Sannox. Once there were many houses here, but the Clearances sent all the inhabitants away, most of them to Canada. Instead of men and women, you now see sheep and deer. The deer are very numerous here, and you should keep your eyes open for the white stag. Another of the many superstitions on Arran is that a white stag will appear when the laird is going to die. This white stag was seen several months before the Duchess of Montrose died, and many people have seen it since.

The mountain scenery is very fine hereabouts and we climb to nearly 600 feet before we descend into Glen Chalmadale and reach Lochranza. There is a big Scottish Youth Hostel here and hotels, shops and a pier which is used throughout the summer by the steamer between Gourock and Campbeltown. Lochranza stands between high hills and doesn't get much sun in the winter time. In the bay are the ruins of Lochranza Castle, once a hunting seat of the Scottish Kings.

A track leading up the hillside north-east of Lochranza takes you to the Cock of Arran. This is a large stone on a boulder-strewn beach and it marks the most northerly point of the island. If you are energetic and don't mind rock-scrambling you can turn west and get back along the coast to Lochranza by a group of ruined cottages. Here lived the great-grandfather of Mr. Harold Macmillan, and the father of the founder of the famous firm of publishers. You can reach these cottages more easily by taking the shore road on the north side of Lochranza Bay.

We go south to Catacol (Gaelic for " the glen of the wild cat ") and pass the " Twelve Apostles," a terrace of 12 little houses. All the places I mention, however small, have their quota of summer visitors, and these visitors regard their own choice as the best resort on Arran. The road south from Catacol runs close to the sea, and across the water is the Kintyre coast. There is a special charm

Arran: Lochranza.

about the west side of Arran, and its enthusiasts are inclined to scoff at the busy east side.

Four miles south of Catacol is Pirnmill, which got its
name from a mill which once stood there and made pirns
(or bobbins) for the great thread-making firm of Coats in

Paisley. At one time the Campbeltown steamer stopped here and visitors were ferried ashore. If you are seeing this coast from the steamer deck you will have noticed the high white houses of Thundergay up on the hillside between Catacol and Pirnmill. They look remote and difficult to get to, but holiday-makers dote on Thundergay too.

On shore we keep south and come to the clachan of Whitefarland, with its palm trees growing in the open. Then charming little Imachar, and down between the hills and the sea to Dougarie Lodge, a shooting-box which is rented for the season. The burn that comes down by the lodge is the Iorsa, and Glen Iorsa (" the glen of the adder ") is the dramatic-looking defile that runs into the mountains.

Now we go round Machrie Bay and at Machrie we can take a road to the left that skirts the Shiskine Valley and joins the String Road through the mountains to Brodick. If we go straight on we come to the Machrie Water and to the left is a moor where you can see the Standing Stones of Tormore. This is the biggest Druid temple to be found on Arran.

The road goes on to Blackwaterfoot on Drumadoon Bay. Now we are in " civilisation " once again, for here is the first licensed hotel to be seen since we left Lochranza, about 20 miles to the north. Blackwaterfoot has a noted golf course and, if you walk round it, you come to the King's Caves. Robert the Bruce had been hiding on Rathlin Island off the Irish coast and waiting for an opportunity to return to Scotland. In 1307 he crossed to Arran and lived in these caves at Blackwaterfoot. The biggest is the King's Cave, and the others are the King's Kitchen, the King's Cellar, and the King's Stable. Some people say that it was here that Robert the Bruce saw the famous spider and, because it would not give up its climb, he decided to go ahead and drive the English out of Scotland. But claims are also made for a cave on Rathlin and another in Galloway. And some spoil-sports say that Bruce didn't see a spider at all.

Fingal is supposed to have used these caves too and at the top of the bay is Drumadoon Point where a standing stone is said to mark the grave of Fingal's daughter.

Behind Blackwaterfoot is the pleasant Shiskine Valley, where Arran's one-time airport was situated. At the village of Shedog you'll see the churchyard where the stone which is supposed to mark St. Molio's grave is kept. St. Molio was the saint who made the Holy Isle holy, and we will be coming to him later.

We carry on round the south of Arran by a dramatic road made on the cliff side. To the right is the Mull of Kintyre, with the island of Davaar guarding Campbeltown. The island near-by, which looks like a spoon upside down, is Sanda and that is the Gaelic word for a spoon. On a clear day you can see Ireland quite plainly. If you can also see the Mountains of Mourne, then it may be going to rain! To the south-east is Ailsa Craig, also known as " Paddy's Milestone " because it's half way between Belfast and Glasgow.

Just off this coast of Arran is supposed to be a fairy island in the style of the one described by J. M. Barrie in *Mary Rose*. The story is that some fairies decided to leave Arran and go to Ireland. But their fairy boat stopped at this island and they went ashore. They have been there ever since. If your steamer cruises round this coast and you see an island, don't land on any account or you may never be able to leave it again.

The Arran shore here has a bad reputation for wrecks. As many as four wrecked ships have been seen at one time on the rockbound coast. It was also a favourite place for smugglers bringing in contraband from Ireland, and that may account for some of the ghost stories told of the area.

By road we traverse the steep hills and glens through Corriecravie to Sliddery. We cross the Sliddery Water (good fishing) and climb towards Lagg. The road to the left is the Ross Road, which crosses Arran to Lamlash and is the highest road on the island. It climbs to almost 1,000 feet and the scenery is reminiscent of the wildest parts of

Skye. As you enter Glen Monamore from the Sliddery end you see the Laird's Bridge, and that's where the notorious Laird of Lagg was killed when he was driving his coach back one night from a mad carouse in Lamlash.

We go down a very steep hill into Lagg (Gaelic for " a hollow,"), which is by far the warmest spot in Arran. It consists of a charming inn and a few cottages, and is completely enclosed. Palms grow in the open, and there is a tea garden in use from spring to autumn. It was here that the Laird of Lagg, who sold his soul to the devil, dug up a skull in a field across the Torlin Water. He put this skull on his sideboard and the whole house started to shake. It went on shaking until he buried the skull again.

You can get down to the beach at Lagg by a pleasant tree-lined path called the Lovers' Walk. Here, when smuggling was rife, two young lovers were mistaken in the summer dim for smugglers and shot by the gaugers.

We climb out of Lagg to Kilmory, where the Milk Marketing Board's creamery is on the right of the road. Here some of the best cheese in Scotland is made. Arran cheese is constantly winning prizes but, unfortunately, it's for export only. You may be able to get it in England more easily than you can in Scotland.

Across the hill we go to Kildonan, by Bennan Head where there is the Black Cavern. It runs into the cliffs for 50 yards and is 80 feet high. There is the customary tale of the piper and his dog going into it, and the piper never coming back but his dog being found many miles away. At certain times, naturally, the piper can still be heard playing in the cave.

A steep road leading off the main road to the right takes us down into Kildonan, where there is a good hotel, several boarding houses, the ruins of a castle, a coastguard station, and Pladda Island just out from the shore. There is a lighthouse on Pladda and holiday-makers take a motor boat across to the island for picnics.

Now the road goes north and dips and rises and dips again, with many twists and turns. Around here was my favourite road notice. It said simply, " Many Dangerous Corners for Miles." But it has disappeared. When Arran Week started, a round-the-island bicycle race was run. There were so many smashes that it has never been run since.

Not far inland from Kildonan is the Black Loch, where a monster dwells. A farmer drove a horse and cart into the loch, and the monster rose and pulled them all below. Only the cart was ever seen again. The last time I visited the Black Loch was on a grey day but, though the loch looked very sinister indeed, the monster did not appear.

From the road we can see the Ayrshire coast to the east. We come round by Dippin Lodge, another shooting-box but one which you'll see better from the water. We go down a long hill into Whiting Bay. Arran's longest pier is at Whiting Bay but it is used mainly in the summer. Behind Whiting Bay is Glen Ashdale, with a two-tiered waterfall that is the highest in Arran. The village has many hotels and a permanent show of Arran arts and crafts in the former St. Columba's Church.

To the north of Whiting Bay is King's Cross Point and it was from here that Robert the Bruce set off for the Carrick shore to start his War of Independence. His men had taken Brodick Castle and he was now waiting for a beacon to be lit on the Ayrshire coast to show that the time was ripe for him to land. On a clear day you can see Turnberry lighthouse, built on the ruins of the castle in which Bruce was born. One night Bruce saw a blaze on the far shore and ordered his ships to cross the Firth. But when they landed they found the beacon had not been lit. Bruce decided to stay and fight, and his fighting ended with the Battle of Bannockburn in June, 1314, when the Scots defeated Edward II and held their own land once more. A cairn at King's Cross Point marks the spot where Bruce embarked.

The road runs across to Lamlash and most of the way we can see the Holy Isle, which protects Lamlash Bay and makes it such a safe anchorage. King Haakon of Norway

remustered his broken fleet in Lamlash Bay after the
Battle of Largs, and then sailed home, never to return.
Today the British Navy use Lamlash Bay as an anchorage.

As we come down the hill to Lamlash we see on the left,
by an old mill, the other end of the Ross Road, descending
steep Glen Scorrodale. Up this glen lived the Giant Scorri,
who terrorised the whole district. The clever men of
Lamlash devised a plan to defeat him. They divided into
two bands and each took a side of the glen. When the first
band sighted Scorri they yelled at the giant and he pursued
them. Just as they vanished into the heather, the men on
the other side of the glen started shouting insults. So the
giant ran down one side of the glen and up the other.
Before he was half way up the hillside, his tormentors had
disappeared and the first group were out again on the
opposite side, taunting him once more. The enraged giant
ran down and then up. The Lamlash men kept up this
tactic until their victim was exhausted. Then they attacked
and slew him, and the Giant Scorri is buried somewhere on
the slopes of Glen Scorrodale.

Just as we enter Lamlash we see on the left the island's
Secondary School. It's built where the famous Donald
Mackelvie experimented with his series of seed potatoes
that are now known throughout the world. Mr. Mackelvie,
who ran a grocer's shop in Lamlash, won the Lord Derby
award for the best new variety of potato eight times, a
record which no other seed potato grower has ever achieved.
He prefixed the name of all his new potatoes with "Arran,"
and Arran Banner, Arran Pilot and Arran Comrade are
three of them.

Lamlash is said to be the biggest village on Arran, though
it must be a very close thing now between its population
and Brodick's. It's a holiday resort without a pier. The old
pier was considered dangerous, and all that is left now is a
jetty for motor boats, puffers and fishing smacks.

A motor boat will take you across Lamlash Bay to the
Holy Isle, which is more than a mile long and 1,030 feet in
height. There is a house on the island but it is not always

Holy Island.

Scottish Tourist Board.

occupied. There's also a lighthouse, and a herd of some-times embarrassingly friendly wild goats. The Holy Isle takes its name from St. Molios (or Maol Jos), a disciple of St. Columba, who lived in the Saint's Cave, 30 feet up from the sea. There are all sorts of inscriptions in this cave, some of them said to be prehistoric, others of Viking origin, and several very modern indeed.

St. Molios is supposed to have lived to the age of 120 years. His well is near the cave and there is a large sandstone rock, with some carved foot and handholds, which is known as the Saint's Chair. It looks as though it had once been a seat of justice.

If you walk to Clauchlands Farm on the north coast of Lamlash Bay, you can take a path up the hill to the vitrified

fort of Dun Finn. From there a track leads down to Corriegills and thence to Brodick.

The main road to Brodick is about three miles long and has some of the finest views in Arran. From the top of the brae, where there are Standing Stones, you look across at the jagged mountains surrounding Goatfell. On a fine day the vista is magnificent.

But the whole Isle of Arran ranges from the magnificent to the merely delightful. No wonder people go back year after year to this enchanting island.

Opposite—Lamlash.

CHAPTER TWELVE

THE FRINGES OF THE FIRTH

THIS chapter is a postscript for those who take the steamer cruises to the fringes of the Firth of Clyde. The three principal cruises are through the Kyles of Bute and up Loch Fyne, from Gourock to Campbeltown by way of Lochranza, and round Ailsa Criag.

I've already taken you through the Kyles of Bute. The steamer turns at Ardlamont Point and goes up Loch Fyne, by far the longest loch in this part of the world. From Ardlamont to its most northerly shore is 42 miles. Loch Fyne is the home of the famous herring, and there are fishery stations at various parts of the loch where the movements of herrings are examined.

As we sail up Loch Fyne the Kintyre coast is to our left. The rocky promontory is Skipness Point and behind it are the ruins of Skipness Castle, yet another fortress belonging once to the Vikings. We sail in to Tarbert pier. The ruined castle behind the pier was occupied by Robert the Bruce in 1326, and the Scottish Parliament met in the town. Tarbert was once a great fishing port, but nowadays it's better known as a holiday resort.

Less than a mile from Tarbert you can stand on the shores of the Atlantic. West Loch Tarbert is a long narrow, arm of the Atlantic, and at one time men dragged their boats across this neck of land to save themselves the trouble of sailing round Kintyre to get to Loch Fyne.

Ardrishaig and entrance to Crinan Canal. 　　　*Scottish Tourist Board.*

North of Tarbert we see the island of Barmore and behind it the mansion is Stonefield House. We sail into Loch Gilp and look north and see far up Loch Fyne to the peaks of Ben Cruachan, 30 miles away. There are twin villages at the top of Loch Gilp—Ardrishaig and Lochgilphead. The pier is at Ardrishaig, and this is usually the turning point of the cruise. Just behind the pier is the Crinan Canal, which runs nine miles to Crinan but is suitable only for yachts and small boats. The two villages are popular with holiday-makers who are satisfied with simple joys and lasting pleasures.

If the steamer goes right up to the top of Loch Fyne, we pass the entrance to Loch Gilp and find that the loch narrows considerably. At its broadest it is only two miles and the hills rise steep on either side. The rocky height on the left is Silvercraigs, so called because silver was found there. Just here is the Otter Spit, a sandbank which comes out from the Cowal shore and narrows the entrance to this part of the loch to three-quarters of a mile.

Just over three miles to the north you see on the left the inlet of Loch Gair, with a village of the same name at its head. Farther on is Minard Castle—Minard means " the smooth height." We thread several rocky little islands and see on the right the ruins of Castle Lachlan, and the modern mansion a little farther up. The address of the laird there is Lachlan Maclachlan of Stra'lachlan, Castle Lachlan, Stra'lachlan, Loch Fyne. If you've managed " It's a braw, bricht, moonlicht nicht," try this one.

On the left we see the granite quarries of Crarae and then Furnace, where an iron-smelting works was established in the 18th century. Then we come to Pennymore House and the clachan of Kenmore. Over on the right we see the

Inveraray.

Scottish Tourist Board.

village of Strachur. The pier is no longer used, but the hotel behind it is Creggans, now owned by Sir Fitzroy Maclean. From Strachur the main road runs south by Loch Eck to Dunoon.

About five miles north from Strachur we see the little village of St. Catherines on our right, and the capital of Argyll, Inveraray, on our left. There is a regular ferry service across the loch between them.

From the water Inveraray has a Spanish air, but on land it looks uncompromisingly Scottish. The Town Cross was brought from Iona and the English translation of the inscription says, " This is the cross of the noble men, namely Duncan MacComyn, Patrick his son, and Ludovick the son of Patrick, who caused this cross to be erected." The main buildings are the County Buildings, where the Sheriff Court sits, and the Parish Church in the town square. This is really two kirks, and the services are conducted in English in one and in Gaelic in the other. A mile-long avenue of fine beeches leads to the Episcopal Church built by a former Duke.

The Duke of Argyll has opened Inveraray Castle to the public and it's worth visiting. Inveraray has belonged to the Argylls since the 14th century, but the present castle was started in 1745 and finished about 1765. The elder Adam designed it, and it's made of slate from the other side of Loch Fyne.

Inveraray Castle.

The hill that overlooks Inveraray Castle is Duni-quoich and the little building on the top was a watch-tower used by the wary Dukes of Argyll to see what strangers were coming up Loch Fyne.

Farther up the loch is Dundarave Castle, made famous as *Doom Castle* by

Neil Munro. Munro was an Inveraray man and there's a great deal about this district in his novel, *John Splendid*.

Right at the top of Loch Fyne the road runs round to the east and the Rest and Be Thankful route to Glasgow.

You can go by road south from Inveraray right down the Kintyre coast to Campbeltown. From the steamer you see the lower part of Kintyre once your vessel turns round the north of Arran and calls at Lochranza before sailing on to Campbeltown. You can't see much of Kintyre from the sea, but you'll be able to make out the villages of Grogport and Carradale.

About nine miles north of Campbeltown is Saddell, where you can see the well preserved Saddell Castle and behind it the remains of Saddell Monastery, built by Somerled of the Isles in the 12th century. There are tombs of warriors, priests and the Lords of the Isles.

We sail into Campbeltown by Davaar Island, which protects the town as the Holy Isle shelters Lamlash. You can go by motor boat to Davaar and see the Crucifixion painting in one of the caves on the sea side of the island. It was painted originally on the bare rock by a Campbeltown artist, Archibald Mackinnon. He went to live in England but in 1934, when he was 80 years of age, he returned to retouch his painting. It is now looked after regularly and is much admired by visitors.

Campbeltown is a pleasant Highland town with a fine green, a good promenade, a busy shopping centre and many hotels. Just as you come off the pier you see a Celtic cross, brought from Iona in the 12th century, with a Latin inscription which reads, " This is the cross of Mr. Edward M. H. Eachran, once rector of Cyregan, and of Mr. Andrew, his son, rector of Kilcoman, who erected this cross."

Dr. Norman Macleod, perhaps the most famous of all Scottish ministers, was born in the old manse here. Burns's Highland Mary lived in the town too, and some people assert that she was born in Campbeltown and not in Dunoon.

The Clyde is the Gateway to the Western Highlands and Islands

MacBrayne's Royal Mail Steamers and Coach Services have long served as a link between the busy Firth of Clyde and the quiet waters and harbours of the West. Steamer services operate daily except Sundays from Gourock via the Kyles of Bute to Tarbert, Loch Fyne (for Islay) and Ardrishaig (for Oban).

Ailsa Craig from the Ayrshire Coast.

Campbeltown can also be reached by air from Renfrew Airport, Glasgow, and this was the very first internal air service to be introduced in Scotland.

Across from the Mull of Kintyre towards the coast of Ayrshire stands the lonely Ailsa Craig, described by the poet Keats as " thou craggy pyramid." It is about two miles round and 1,114 feet high. Until recently the granite for the curling stones made at Mauchline was quarried here, and these stones are said by experts to be the finest in the world. You can still land on Ailsa Craig where, beside the lighthouse, there is a tea room and an old watch-tower. Apart from the lighthouse staff there are rats, rabbits, wild goats and multitudes of sea birds.

With Ailsa Craig we reach our farthest fringe of the Firth of Clyde. May I end this book by wishing you fair weather for your voyages round the Firth? Providence and the people of this part of the world have supplied everything else that you need for a happy holiday.